FREEDOM'S JOURNEY

DENNIS A. MCINTYRE

BENNETT
MEDIA & MARKETING

FREEDOM'S JOURNEY

Copyright © 2011 by Dennis A. McIntyre

This is a work of fiction. All of the characters, names, incidents, organizations, and dialogue in this novel are either the products of the author's imagination or are used fictitiously.

Bennett books may be ordered through booksellers or by contacting:

Bennett Media and Marketing
1603 Capitol Ave., Suite 310 A233
Cheyenne, WY 82001
www.thebennettmediaandmarketing.com
Phone: 1-307-202-9292

ISBN: 978-1-957114-12-5 (sc)
ISBN: 978-1-957114-13-2 (e)

Printed in the United States of America

Bennett Media rev. date: 03/31/2022

ABOUT THE AUTHOR

D ennis A. McIntyre is a native of Rochester, NY, and served as an electrical engineer and a technical writer for over 40 years before retiring. Since retirement, Dennis has focused his efforts on his personal writing, publishing his first book, an autobiographical work entitled *Legacy of Love*, in 2008 through Tate Publishing. Dennis currently resides in Dacula, GA, and attends Anchor Church in Grayson, GA. He enjoys using his gifts of encouraging and writing for the glory of God's kingdom. His main goal for writing involves drawing people into closer relationships with the Lord and one another.

This work is a continuation of Jake Wilson's story from "Shackled but Free."

Contents

DENNIS A. MCINTYRE

THE ADJUSTMENT

The Wilson family had suddenly outgrown their three-bedroom apartment. Jake and Terry entered the courthouse as a family of four and left as parents for two more, namely Alicia and Nicole. Jake hoped to increase his visitation privileges with the girls in his custody battle with his ex-wife, Joan, but God had a different plan. In a few weeks, the paperwork would make everything official, and the Wilson household would have three daughters and a son.

Jake's dark colored butch hair cut complimented his chiseled, battle-scarred face. Although you might feel a bit fearful on a first encounter, his firm handshake and captivating smile would relieve the tension quickly. Terry, on the other hand, made you feel like you had known her for years. Her medium length blonde hair, piercing blue eyes, and radiance was like a warm beacon of light. They were deeply in love and devoted to each other, family, and God. To friends, they were the perfect family. Yet, for them, the road ahead was filled with uncertainty. Their apartment was cramped for a family of four and now there were six. Jake's work as a plumber was touch and go. The work was plentiful, but without a plumber's license, many jobs were not available for Jake's bid.

Matt (Matthew) and Diana were children from Terry's first marriage and adopted by Jake after he married her. Their last names were changed to Wilson, so the additions of Nicole and Alicia were a welcomed fit. The name "Wilson" carried a family bond. Both Jake and Terry reflected on all that had happened with a sense of awe. Terry came out of an abusive marriage, and Jake overcame his lawless past. Together, they had formed a family centered on the faith that their union was not accidental. God had worked a miracle in bringing them together. Now, the blessings of adding Nicole and Alicia to the mix, was like an exclamation point.

Nicole and Alicia had auburn hair like their mother. Matt and Diana's hair was blonde like their mom. They were different in appearance, but that's as far as it went. There was a genuine love for each other.

Nicole and Alicia had been treated like family for eight years prior to the court's decision, as they spent many weekends at the Wilson household. The girls were close in age and enjoyed many of the same activities together. Matt was the little brother. Diana was the oldest at fourteen. Alicia was thirteen, Nicole twelve, and Matt just enjoyed his eleventh birthday. Matt's birthday took on special significance, as it marked a two-month period when they would be one year in age apart. Alicia's birthday would mark a four-month period when she and Diana would be the same age. In short, the children seemed to draw great strength from each other.

On one occasion, the girls were discussing their ages with some half-hearted humor. Diana began the conversation with the fact that she was the oldest.

"Look at this Alicia and 'Nicki.' (Nicole had picked up this nickname from the others). Our initials starting from the oldest to the youngest are 'DANM.' I'm so glad that Matt wasn't born before Nicki. Aren't you?"

The girls wrote the letters as 'DAMN' to identify that scenario and laughed hysterically. Matt heard the commotion and went to the girl's room to inquire. They shared the thought process with him, and he laughed as well. They were a bunch of well-adjusted kids. Laughter was as normal as breathing to them. The sound of it was equally pleasing to Terry and Jake, when he was home to hear it.

Dinnertime together was equally enjoyable. Jake made it a point to complete his plumbing work by six to ensure that he was home for the evening meal. Terry was a great cook, but Jake especially enjoyed the camaraderie around the dinner table. Not only did he listen with great intent to each child's events for the day, but they were just as eager to share as well. Jake had become the father, that he never had, to Matt and the girls. Except for a few emergencies, the plumbing business was over when Jake came through the door at night.

Jake's role as husband meant providing for his family. But, his role as father took on greater significance. He never really knew his father as a child growing up. A teenage affair with a married woman resulted in a son, named Brandon, which constantly tugged at Jake's heartstrings. His brief marriage with Brandon's mother ended with divorce, along with all communication. His ex-wife moved out of the state and was never heard from again. Jake's heart pounded even more since his spiritual conversion. Parental responsibility as a teenager was something foreign, but now it is everything.

Terry had many late night discussions with her husband after Jake woke up in a heavy sweat from bad dreams. The dreams always involved his son, Brandon. Jake would have many thoughts and questions like:

> *"I wonder where my son is today?"*
> *"I hope he is being raised by a good caring family"*
> *"Do you think he knows about his father?"*
> *"Does he have any of my features?"*

Brandon's life was like a dark hole in Jake's heart. Abandonment seems to leave an emptiness, which Jake knew all too well. Jake also knew that holes needed to be filled. God had done that for him. Guilt and shame had marked Jake's life until the Lord got hold of him. The transformation resulted in joy and peace, except for one last scar. Thoughts of Brandon still surfaced, though mostly through dreams. It was as if God was not done with Jake's restoration process. Ephesians 2:10 continually reminded Jake that he was a work in progress. Still, the dreams persisted.

The weights, of providing for a family, being a good husband, and nurturing the children, weighed heavily on Jake. The apartment was too small, but home ownership did not seem to be a realistic possibility. Jake's incarceration, although a decade ago, would still be a hindrance. Being self-employed as an unlicensed plumber didn't help much either, not to mention the roller coaster workload. There had been many months where the monies for their tithing check would not be deposited until the eleventh hour. Yet, God was always faithful. Applying for a mortgage with a banking institution might not offer the same measure of faith, however.

Still. Jake was a man at peace. The burdens for Nicole and Alicia had been lifted in a mighty way. Jake feared for their very lives, while they were under their mother's control. Terry treated them as her own, right from the first time they had a stay over. Matt and Diana seemed to accept them as sisters as well. It was magical and surreal. The life Jake knew before his spiritual conversion was a radical difference from the one he now enjoyed. Yes, there was real peace and a certainty that God was in control in Jake's life.

Terry also felt relief. The welfare of Jake's daughters had been like a millstone around Jake's neck for eight years. Now, the weight had been lifted. No longer did Jake carry the burden. Terry's role as mother for Alicia and Nicole came naturally. She truly loved them as her own, and her love for Jake grew in proportion. She felt God's hand in her life as well.

THE MEN'S GROUP

A local non-denominational church had become an integral part of the Wilson family's life. Sunday mornings meant an hour of Bible study and a message to follow in a service. The children had their programs as well. Nicole and Alicia experienced the procedure before, during their weekend visits and enjoyed the new friendships. Sunday was also the one day that Jake did not work, except for a rare emergency. Even during those times, his family supported him.

Wednesday evening offered additional worship times for everyone. Jake enjoyed listening to a Bible scholar's dissertations along with the fellowship around the coffee and pastry section of the church. Paul also looked forward to meeting with Jake there. Paul led a Bible study on Thursday night at another church in the area, where they first met. The two men had become great friends, with many of the same interests. Paul was self-employed as well, and the downturn in the economy had taken its financial toll for them both. Throughout the week, their cell phones would be interactive with similar requests.

"Hey, Paul. You're buddy Jake here. Business is slow. I need your prayers friend."

"Ditto, Jake. So what's goin'on? How are the kids getting along?"

"The girls spend a lot of time laughing together. I have to tell them to close their bedroom door. Don't get me wrong, buddy, it's wonderful."

"They seem to carry that enthusiasm to church as well. I've heard them giggling."

"Matt enjoys his role as the little brother as well. Sometimes he antagonizes the girls and then leaves. You can always tell by the smirk on his face, afterwards."

"That's typical, for the youngest child, Jake."

"Yeah! I think the girls know what's going on in the exchange. I have heard Matt's name mentioned during some of those laughter outbursts."

"So, it sounds like things are going well with the kids."

"I cannot imagine a better relationship than they have. It is wonderful to watch."

"I envy you, Jake. We have but one son. He's a great kid, but I wonder at times, whether having more children would have been better for his sake."

"Hayden is a great young man, Paul. I have seen him with the others in his Wednesday youth group. You do not have to worry about him."

"Yeah! Still...anyway, what's going on in the plumbing business?"

"You know, up then down. It's a fact of life. Pray for a couple of large bids that I have on the table. If I land at least one of them, I will have work for several months. It sure would help if I had my license."

"Same here, Jake. I need a really strong month to complete the quarter, and the phone has not been ringing lately."

"It will, Paul. You need to have faith. God has never let me down since I gave my life to him."

"I see how He has answered your prayers, my friend, but I think He answers mine differently."

"Yeah, well…Paul, I think you worry too much. This call is more of a courtesy call. Although I believe many prayers are better than one, I want you to know that I love you as my friend."

"Ditto."

Paul and Jake had an open dialog on a regular basis. Paul continued to lead the Thursday night study, which Jake regularly attended. Their fellowship was a necessary part of their daily activities. Jake had fellowship before he gave his heart to the Lord, but it came in the form of gang members. He had the "I got your back" mentality and knew there was power in numbers. His Christian walk, however, needed others as accountability partners. Men need other men for those tasks. Both men knew that old behaviors could pop up, and that a spiritual war was being waged against them. Fighting temptations was difficult alone. Paul needed Jake and vice versa.

The Thursday men's group usually had between six and ten attendees. The format started with about ten minutes of "What's happening?" discussions, where men openly shared about things that transpired since their last meeting. It was during these times that new prayer needs surfaced. It was especially good for newcomers to participate in those moments. When Jake first attended, he was overwhelmed with the concerns from the others as he shared about his life. His first visit did not ask for prayers for personal needs, but the men did so anyway. You could say that they had his back. He rarely missed a Thursday meeting. He knew that having Christian brothers was a vital ingredient to living and doing the Lord's will. After receiving custody of his daughters, Jake could not wait to share his joy with his brothers.

"Hey, Jake. What's happening? Your smile tells me you had a good week."

"Good is not the word Paul. This has been a great week."

"Tell us more. How'd your court meeting go?"

"You guys are the best. I think God answered your prayers for me beyond even your dreams."

"Come on buddy. Don't keep us in suspense here."

"I won custody of Alicia and Nicole. I mean, they are living with me as we speak."

"How did that happen?"

"That's a really long story, starting with the judge who had me imprisoned. Let's just say that God worked out every detail."

"You have got to share a little more than that. Let's see...Joan was a respected police officer and you were a convicted felon. Something must have changed for you to get custody. Does that mean you don't have to pay child support? What about her visitation rights?"

"Child support is a done deal. Joan needs to get rehabilitated for substance and child abuse to have any rights in the future. I am telling you that God worked out everything."

"He must have, Jake."

"Nicole and Alicia are really enjoying their time with Matt and Diana as well. I am telling you that I floated out of that courtroom. My feet never touched the floor."

"That explains it."

"Explains what?"

"When you came in, I thought you were ten feet tall. Your eyes were bluer than the Caribbean waters and sparkled like diamonds."

Everyone in the group laughed together and shared in Jake's joy. The fellowship was infectious to two new attendees as well. Introductions were made so that the new arrivals could feel at home. They had not met Jake before that night, but could not escape the spirit in that room. Paul opened the meeting with a word of prayer, in which he thanked God for the answers He provided on behalf of Jake. Then he opened by soliciting new prayer concerns or praises from the men.

As each regular attendee shared, the new guests listened intently. They came to a Bible study with the evening's topic that night on "A Father's Role." Jake's story was a perfect lead-in, along with several of the men's prayer requests and concerns. One quest was a father of two young boys. The other was anticipating fatherhood with his wife seven months along. One had questions about leadership, while the other came in with a need for a "Fatherhood for Dummies" book.

Paul could not get over the timing of Jake's story and the subject for discussion. He often spent many hours wondering how to get the men in his group to open up. He even agonized over it at times. Just like that, the ice was broken. The men entered the discussion readily, even the newcomers. The Holy Spirit was at work.

Jake anticipated something special would occur in those Thursday meetings, and was rarely disappointed. He had learned the importance of regular gathering of believers, especially men, for spiritual and emotional edification. Like women, men wear many hats. They are providers, spiritual leaders in their homes, fathers, husbands, and much more. Trying to perform all of these tasks alone is nearly impossible and often foolish. Thursdays for Jake was like recharging his batteries for the power needed each week.

DENNIS A. MCINTYRE

CUSTODY SECURED

D uring the court settlement, Judge Anthony Carter informed Jake that there would be some finalization papers to be signed, and that his office would let him know when to come in. The papers arrived, and Jake returned to the courthouse with his family to seal the deal. There was something concrete about knowing that everything would be legally settled. The thought, that Joan might find a way to block the court's decision, was still on Jake's mind.

"Hi Jake," Judge Carter shouted after he entered the room.

"Hi Judge."

"This should only take a few minutes, Jake. Have a seat, while I have the court stenographer come in as a witness."

"Thanks Judge. You know how I love these leather chairs."

"Yeah, me too. They're comfortable and I love the smell. So how are you girls doing?"

Nicole and Alicia smiled. Three weeks had passed since the last time they were in that office. The smiles on their faces said it all, but they still managed to respond with:

"Great."

"What about you Mrs. Wilson? The girls appear to be well adjusted."

"You can just call me Terry, Judge."

"Okay, Terry,"

"I'm fine, sir. Everyone gets along wonderfully. It is a pleasure being a mom for each of them."

"It shows on your face."

"You have confirmed my decision from three weeks ago as the right one."

Just then two stenographers entered the room.

"Now Jake, we have a few forms to sign, giving you full custody and all legal rights as Nicole and Alicia's guardian. Your ex-wife's rights will be terminated until another court reinstates them. At any rate, she can only petition for visitation. How does that sound to you?"

"Like a dream, sir. It's like a dream. The girls now have a home filled with love."

"Yeah! I can see that."

"Have you talked with your father since we met last, Judge?"

"I called him that weekend. Your case really had an emotional affect on me."

"How's that, sir?"

"Over the years, we had our ups and downs. I always wished my dad had spent more time with me. He worked a lot. I think we talked more on that weekend than in our entire life. He had always been there for me, but I judged him by quantity and not quality time sent. My friends had far more quantity time and I was, well jealous.

"So you guys got re-acquainted, huh?"

"That we did, Jake. Thank you for asking."

"I really like the old guy, Judge."

"Me too, but don't let him hear you refer to him as 'old.'"

"He was like a father to me as well, sir."

"And many more like you. That was what I had to learn. His quality time was far more precious than all my friends' quantity time with their dads. It was as though my dad was called to a mission of service."

"I truly believe that as well, sir."

"Now sign where I made the highlights, and we can make this official."

Jake proceeded to complete all the documents and received a copy. The court would make raised-sealed copies for Jake as well, but the signatures from the witnesses made everything official.

"Thank you Judge,"

"Thank you as well Jake Wilson."

DENNIS A. MCINTYRE

COOKIE DOUGH

The Wilson's kitchen was a special bonding place for their family. The aroma of a great home cooked meal permeated the entire house, drawing each member into the room for a closer look or pre-taste. Terry often asked Matt and Diana if they would like to help her in the kitchen. Diana nearly always responded eagerly, but Matt was more at ease playing video games in his room. That is, until the work involved making chocolate chip cookies. Sibling rivalry would take place over who licks the beaters or gets to sample the uncooked dough first.

Now, such an event would involve Nicole and Alicia as well. They had never experienced anything like that before. Cooking usually involved the delivery of fast food, and clean up often took days. Terry's kitchen was always spotless after the work was completed. She insisted, and the children had their chores to perform to ensure that everything was put back in their rightful place afterwards. Nicole and Alicia witnessed their new brother and sister performing their chores without complaining and thought that was somewhat unusual. Nevertheless, when they were asked to help make cookies, they eagerly volunteered.

Baking cookies was a process. Terry could have made them much quicker without any help, but desired to pass on the knowledge she learned from her mother to her children. She was excited to see Nicole and Alicia's willingness to pitch in. It was a way for the girls to further blend into the family unit, so the extra hour or two, that it would take, was well worth the effort. There was one minor problem, however. The same amount of cookie dough needed to make four-dozen cookies almost doubled, not because of excessive waste, but due to consumption. Nicole and Alicia had not had the opportunity to taste uncooked dough before. They found that they really enjoyed it.

> *"Hey Matt. Pass the dough over here,"* Diana shouted.
> *"If I do that, we won't have any left for cookies."*
> *"What do you mean?"* Alicia asked.
> *"I mean, she will eat it all up."*
> *"No way. You don't eat uncooked cookie dough, do you?"*
> *"You bet! It's great. You should try it,"* Diana responded.
> *"Sounds gross."*
> *"I'll try some,"* Nicole added and dipped her pointing finger into the dough. *"Ummm. That's really yummy. I can't believe I never tried it before. Try some Alicia"*
> *"That's sick. There's raw eggs in there."*
> *"Come on and try it sis. You'll like it."*
> *"Just a small taste and you'll be hooked,"* Diana added.
> *"I suppose I will have to try spinach later as well."*
> *"I like spinach,"* Matt blurted.
> *"You do want to be part of this family, don't you Alicia. We can be bound together by cookie dough."*
> *"I guess that would be better than blood, Diana. OK, but just a small taste."*

Diana dipped her finger into the dough and placed it in front of Alicia's mouth. Alicia thought about holding her nose to, somehow, prevent the anticipated raunchy taste from reaching her taste buds, but decided to get the matter over quickly. To her surprise, it went down much better than she had thought.

"Wow! That really does taste good. Am I officially part of the family now?"

"Oh Alicia. You already were," Matt inserted. *"We were just playing with you."*

"But, whenever I think of cookie dough, especially chocolate chip, I can recall this moment as our time of bonding together."

"Me too," Nicole added. *"Me too."*

Terry could not stop the tears from gently flowing down her cheek. She began to make up another batch of dough, knowing that the quantity of baked cookies was about to be severely diminished. The children enjoyed that time together in the kitchen. Terry enjoyed it even more. Whenever she wanted to get the kids together and away from video games or television, all she had to do was suggest making cookies. She tried other flavors, but chocolate chip was by far the children's all-time favorite.

There was something else going on in that kitchen that may not have been as apparent as the joy on each child's face. Nicole and Alicia had found a peaceful place to rest their heads. Terry did not know what went on when these girls were with their mother. She saw anguish on their faces at times, but the looks quickly faded when they spent the night on those occasions in the past. She did not know that these girls were verbally abused any time they left their rooms, except for school, meals, or bathroom breaks. Nicole and Alicia were kept out of sight and out of mind, whenever Joan had guests over, which was nearly every night. Baking cookies was not on Joan's agenda. Besides, you can buy two-pound bags of them for less cost.

Each time the kids spent together helping in the kitchen was part of an emotional healing process. The bad dreams that Nicole and Alicia had before became less frequent. Although, they were doing well in school, their grades slowly improved even more. More school friends were invited home with them. It was as if God invented chocolate chip cookie dough as a natural remedy for their pent up emotional healing.

Terry would share the exploits of the children in the kitchen with Jake over dinner. She would barely start talking, when each child would interrupt with his or her own interpretation. Those dinner times were filled with heavy doses of laughter. Although, Jake wasn't there as an eyewitness, he certainly shared in the experience. Those times were especially heartwarming for Terry and Jake. "We're doing good," they would think and then pass along to each other through eye contact. Without words, the message was received loud and clear. Healing was going on in the Wilson family to be sure and God was in it.

A NEW DREAM

The Wilson family of six was packed liked sardines in their three-bedroom apartment. Jake's plumbing business took the bulk of additional space in the one car garage that came with the rental. The children were going through growth spurts that demanded even more storage space for new wardrobes. Jake and Terry talked at great length about finding a place that would meet their growing needs, but the options seemed few and far between.

Having a home of their own would, certainly, be the answer, but qualifying for a loan offered significant problems. Jake's business was meeting their bills, but cash flow was like a roller coaster. Jake would land large contracts with new homebuilders, which would provide several months of continuous work. But, payment might come thirty, sixty, or even ninety days after each phase was completed. Filling out the bank forms regarding monthly income was difficult, and Jake's business records needed a CPA to decipher. Nevertheless, Terry and Jake were hopeful. God had brought them together, answered their prayers for the girls, and met their physical needs so far.

"Terry, are you awake?"
"I'm awake. What's up?"
"I'm having trouble falling asleep tonight."
"What's the matter? You know you can talk to me anytime, honey."

"I know sweetheart. You're always there for me and I really appreciate it. The kids are getting so big."

"That's what kids do," Terry said with a sheepish grin.

"I know that, but this place isn't growing. Three girls in one bedroom as teenagers is not a comforting thought. They need more space."

"I have thought a lot about that, too. Right now, they seem to be content, however."

"Yeah! They're terrific. Still, I dream about being a better provider for you and the kids."

"You are a great provider. No one is complaining, especially not me. Things will work out. You'll see."

"God has opened a lot of doors in my life. I guess I should wait on Him a bit more, huh?"

"Why don't we ask Him to open up one more door, Jake?"

"Like a house?"

Terry and Jake prayed together, asking God to provide a way to have a place with adequate room for their family. Jake felt at peace afterwards and quickly fell asleep. Terry felt her husband's warm embrace and just as quickly heard a gentle snoring. She reached over and picked up the Bible on her nightstand. Jake may have found the relief that he needed, but Terry was fully awake. She opened the Bible to the Proverbs and began to read, trusting that God would provide inspiration. She desperately wanted to support Jake and ease his concerns. She began reading from chapter thirty. Then a few verses seemed to come alive, as if God meant them just for her.

> 24 *"Four things on earth are small,*
>   *yet they are extremely wise:*
> 25 *Ants are creatures of little strength,*
>   *yet they store up their food in the summer;*
> 26 *coneys are creatures of little power,*
>   *yet they make their home in the crags;*

27 locusts have no king,
        yet they advance together in ranks;
28 a lizard can be caught with the hand,
        yet it is found in kings' palaces.

Proverbs thirty was not one of David or Solomon's writings. A wise man named Agur penned the words. Solomon asked for the gift of wisdom and God provided people like Agur to provide it. Often we may find what we are looking for in the least likely places. Agur's words somehow penetrated Terry's heart. She knew all about ants and lizards, as both creatures were in abundance in Central Florida where they lived. Somehow, God had placed a great measure of wisdom upon these creatures and the concept gripped Terry's thoughts.

"What wisdom could come from these critters?" she thought. Ants have little strength, _yet_ they store up their food in the summer. She pictured small morsels of bread being carried away by rows of ants, which fell between the cracks of the picnic table at the nearby park that summer. The food looked much bigger than the ants, yet they were on a mission. Nothing would keep them from their goal. She wondered about the process of gathering food as being about wisdom. It seemed to be more about survival.

Then God opened her eyes to the concept that gathering food while it was plentiful, meant that the colony would have plenty when food was not available. Winter was a long period of time, especially for ants. They would, surely, die without food, but saving up during the good times meant they would have enough to survive the bad. Unlike many humans, the ants knew that they had to work together to gather food while it was in abundance. They could not rest and assume that food would always be available. They were created with the perseverance necessary to carry on the task at hand, despite their limited strength.

When times are going well, many people look towards having more toys or a better vehicle. The idea of saving may have been instilled in the generations of grandparents, but affluence seems to breed even more desires in societies today. Terry thought a while about the wisdom of the ant. Jake's business had many ups and downs. During the good times, Jake talked about buying a bigger and newer truck. He justified the payments as being only slightly higher than the ones he was making on his four-year-old vehicle, which was only a year from being paid off. The difference was an additional six years of writing the checks.

Terry had been supportive of each decision Jake made in the past, but the lesson of the ant told her that she needed to take a stand regarding taking on more debt. Jake worked hard to provide for his family. During the up times, Terry knew that she had to use the wisdom of the ants to save. If a home was in their future, then building a solid savings account needed to be done. Soup and sandwiches filled the belly as well as steak.

Then she began to wonder about the lizards living in palaces. What was God trying to tell her in these words? Matt often brought salamanders, which he had caught in the yard, into his bedroom. The bedroom may have seemed like a palace, but she was sure that was not the meaning of the scripture. Kings were associated with palaces, and guests were very selective. Surely, the king would not seek out the lowly lizard to be a guest. The lizard, though small, knew it could find refuge in the palace. In short, it was the lizard that did the seeking.

God impressed wisdom on Terry that night. First, she needed to help build savings, especially during the good times in Jake's business. Second, she needed to help Jake understand that teamwork was needed to achieve any worthwhile goal. Third, they needed to continually stay in God's presence, which meant bringing their concerns to Him, daily. After thanking God for the new insights, she placed the Bible back on the stand, and went to sleep.

Terry got up the next morning to prepare breakfast. It was a beautiful morning. The sunrise was spectacular. She opened the curtains to get a better view of the golden hue on the horizon. Then she slid the window up to feel the cool morning breeze. A small newt jumped on the window ledge and seemed to look directly at her. It was a moment as if time was standing still. The thoughts Terry had, prior to resting her head on the pillow, came back. The kitchen, suddenly, became a palace. Terry accepted Christ as her Lord eight years earlier. God had found a dwelling place in her heart. Wherever she was, so was God. The newt held its pose for several seconds and then jumped off the ledge. Terry continued to stare at the empty ledge for some time. It was an uplifting moment.

"Breakfast is about ready, honey."

"Thanks. It sure smells good. Did you sleep well?"

"I went to sleep late, but I woke up refreshed."

"I remember sharing something with you, but the next thing I remember was waking up. I dreamed about moving to a bigger house."

"That was the topic of our conversation, so you probably woke up with it still on your mind."

"I guess that makes sense. I would like to provide more living space for my family. Anyway, I must have been dead tired. I hope I wasn't babbling."

"You did fall asleep rather quickly, honey, but we prayed together. Do you remember that?"

"Sort of. I must have been in some sort of trance. Things have been pretty hectic lately. I've had a lot on my mind."

Terry gently placed her hands on Jake's shoulders and began to pray for God's grace. Jake followed with a prayer for his family and the food that had been prepared before him. Terry was especially anxious to see what new insights God had for her that day.

The lesson of the ants had a special significance to Terry. After the kids were off to school, she sat down at the freshly cleaned kitchen table with a notepad and pen. Up to this point, Terry had let the bill paying duties for Jake, but she felt compelled to write down expenditures in three columns. The first row was for essentials like electricity, water, car payments, and rent. Then she added a row for non-monthly payments like car insurance (paid semi-annually), garbage pickup (quarterly), and medical bills. The last column was for future desires. The first item she listed was a bigger home. Then she added items like new wardrobes for the kids, a new vehicle, and a washing machine.

The list of essential items began to grow as items like gasoline, food, and vehicle maintenance were given estimates. Expenditures for each entry were then totaled. Quarterly, semi-annual, and annual items were given monthly equivalents to create a reasonable budget. The list was completed using the previous twelve months of expenses. Terry stared for a moment at the bottom line numbers, while reflecting upon the lesson of the ants. Some months had higher costs due to the weather patterns, like electricity, while other items stayed consistent. The income for each month was volatile as well, due to Jake's roller coaster workload.

Holiday times seemed to offer a greater potential for income as well as a substantial increase in spending for non-essentials. The idea of gathering food in the summer to sustain a long winter for ants could be viewed as putting away more of the profits during the holiday seasons, instead of wishful spending. Large ticket items were being purchased shortly after a windfall month in Jake's business. The gifts may have felt good to each receiver, but did they outweigh the agony during the slow times?

The ants knew what their mission was and now so did Terry. The dream of owning a home began to take root for the first time. Terry completed the spreadsheet of expenses and then asked God to bless her plans to be a better steward.

THE FARMHOUSE

Jake had a busy schedule that day, which included restoration of two bathrooms in an old farmhouse. One of the contractors at the development site, where Jake had lined up about three months worth of work, asked him to give a quote for the farmhouse renovation.

"Hey, Jake. How's your workload?" Bob Peters inquired.

"I'm good for a couple of months, Bob, but you know me. I could always use more."

"You're a worker, Jake. I'll say that for you, and you do good work at that."

"Thanks. I do my best."

"The reason I asked, is that I just inherited a farm about eight miles from here. My aunt passed away about a year ago. Anyway, I am not sure what to do with it. The cattle have all been sold, and the property is beginning to get a bit rundown."

"A farm? Somehow, I don't picture you as a farmer."

"Me neither, but Aunt Bertha must have liked me. She lost her only son in a freak accident several years before she died. I would come over to help her when I could, which was almost weekly. That

old farmhouse was way too big for her, but it was the only home she ever knew."

"You mean she lived alone?"

"For about two years after her husband died. He was in his seventies."

"So how can I help you?"

"The plumbing is all original, Jake. The house has very little copper or plastic piping, and drainage is pretty poor. If I sell it, then I need to modernize it. The land is worth a pretty penny, so fixing it up sounds like a good investment, don't you think?"

"I'd be glad to look at it for you, Bob. Write down the address, and let me know when I can meet you there."

"I was hoping you would say that. Rather than writing it down, how 'bout we go there over lunch? I'll buy the burgers."

"Sounds like a plan to me." The idea of a burger sounded pretty good as well.

The noon whistle blew, and Jake left his worksite to locate Bob. The two men picked up a couple of burgers to go from a nearby chain, and headed up to the farm. Jake barely had time to eat his sandwich, when they arrived. Bob stopped his truck at a gate to unlock the padlock and swing it open. Then they drove down a long gravel-covered drive to an old white house.

The paint appeared to be flaking in a few places, but otherwise was in pretty good condition. The roof looked relatively new, as there was little evidence of soot damage from the chimney. The old sculptured roof supports, which surrounded the house, were especially appealing to Jake's eyes. They seemed out of place for Florida's more modern look.

"Pretty big place you got here, Bob."

"Yeah! A lot of memories here, too, Jake."

"That roof looks new."

"Hurricane Charley in 2004 did my aunt and uncle a favor there. The old roof was on its last legs, when Charley decided to help out.

Anyway, the whole roof was replaced, including most of the wood. The barn's roof was also replaced."

Jake turned towards the barn as Bob spoke. It looked almost as big as the house. Bob decided to give Jake a tour before entering the house to view the plumbing. It was no longer a place for cattle, horses, or an occasional pig, yet the evidence was still there. Stairs led up to a huge loft area, half-filled with bales of straw.

"See that straw, Jake? I used to come here with my parents and make that my sanctuary. Playing hide and seek with my brother and sister was especially fun."

"I didn't know you had any brothers or sisters, I figured your parents would stop cold after having you," Jake responded with a wide smirk on his face.

"They did," Bob responded in kind. *"Joe and Tara are older than me."*

"Did they share in your inheritance?"

"Joe is a minister in Alabama, and Tara married a Canadian. She lives there. I guess my aunt felt that this place should go to me, since I am close by. My name was the only one mentioned at the reading of her will. Joe could turn this ol' barn into a church sanctuary, however."

"It sure is big."

Jake scanned the interior of the barn for several moments, while other thoughts passed through his head. This place could be a great place to build his plumbing business. The barn could hold tons of pipes, tools, and other hardware. Working out of his garage and truck was so limiting in comparison to the potential all around him.

"Let's check out the house, Jake."

"Lead the way."

The house had a back entrance facing the barn, which was about one hundred feet away. The stony path was filled with tall growth, as evidence that it had not been traveled for a while. Inside the door was another storage room filled with crates, empty jars and other collections. Then the door opened to the old kitchen. Jake noticed the outdated appliances, plank flooring, old flowery wallpaper, and tall wooden cabinets in need of restoration. Except for a small bag of trash on the floor, the room was not cluttered, however.

"Take a look at that sink. Isn't it a beauty?" Bob chuckled, as it had seen better days.

"You inherited more than a farm my friend. You got yourself an antique store here."

"Do you think I could sell it that way? Or, would I get a better class of people in with a few modern conveniences like copper pipes, new drain lines, and say a dishwasher."

"It certainly has great potential, but I'd say needs a lot of work. New piping, faucets, dishwasher, and water that flows beyond a trickle would do well." Jake said that as he opened the kitchen faucet up fully. The water, not only came out very slowly, but it was brown in color.

"I guess people would like to at least see clear water, huh?"

"I assume this place is on a well, based on the flow."

"It's in the back. You passed it on the walk from the barn."

Jake proceeded to check out the well, along with the rest of the plumbing needs throughout the house. It had one bathroom upstairs with five large rooms. The downstairs had a small bathroom, without a tub or shower. The dining room looked like it could serve a football team, along with a living room and den. It was a stark contrast from Jake's three-bedroom apartment.

"So work up some ideas for me, Jake. I would like a complete modern plumbing system with new hardware. I also received a little money in the inheritance and feel that Bertha would like to see it go to good use."

"I'll work up a per room price for you along with the costs to upgrade the pumping system at the well. I will need to do some digging in the yard to update that area."

"You let me know what you need, Jake. I will decide what to do from that."

"I will have it for you by the end of the week. How soon do you want to start, assuming that I get the work?"

"I am in no real hurry. I have a lot to do on the property outside the house, anyway. I look forward to your estimate."

The two men went back to the development. Thoughts of the renovation filled Jake's mind. Complete restoration would take about two weeks time after all the materials were at hand. To complete the estimate, Jake would need to contact the county about well restrictions and permits. There was something about that farm that began to permeate Jake's mind and heart. Jake's apartment would fill a portion of the old farmhouse's downstairs. The thought of finishing off the upstairs as bedrooms for each child seemed to fill Jake's mind as he drove home that night. Could this house to God's answer to his prayers?

"Supper sure smells good, sweetie," Jake said as he wrapped his arms around Terry, while she stood facing the kitchen sink.

"You're in a special mode tonight, dear. Having a good day?"

"I had better than a good day. It was great. I may have picked up another good job."

"Wonderful, honey. Now sit down for dinner and we can discuss our days events as a family."

"What's for supper?

"Good home cooking. Now sit."

"Yes, Ma'am."

The kids were already waiting at the table. They helped mom prepare some of the food and couldn't wait to eat. Italian food was held in high esteem at the Wilson house. Terry's Lasagna received the highest compliments along with Texas toast style garlic bread, corn on the cob, and homemade applesauce. A brownie or two for desert didn't hurt either. Alicia couldn't wait to say grace so everyone could dig in.

"So kids, how was school today?" Jake was ready to talk about his time on the farm, but had to take a back seat, while each child shared.

"I made a new friend today," Diana began. *"His name is Steven. He is in my English class."*

"Tell us about him," Terry responded.

"He's really nice and cute too." Jake sat up with a look that implied that he needed to prepare for a possible dating process,

"Cute, huh?" Terry said with a smile.

"Oh, mom. He's adorable. I don't usually enjoy English classes, but I think I will enjoy this one."

"So you are friends," Jake responded. *"Make sure that you keep it at that level."*

"Oh, Dad. You worry too much. We enjoy just talking. Steven is new to the area. He came from Maine, due to his father's work. I like learning about other places besides Florida."

Jake sat back for a moment. Diana called him *"Dad,"* as she had done many times before. Yet, each time brought a sense of pride and joy to his heart. He adopted her along with Matt after marrying their mother. The tumultuous relationship they had with their biological father left bitter scars. Jake truly loved all of his children. He had not given up on having one together with Terry as well. Being accepted as "Dad" meant everything. Along with it came a building trust. Somehow, Diana convinced him that her relationship with Steven was truly okay.

"What about the rest of you kids? Anyone else have something to share?

"I dissected a frog today," Nicole added. *"It was pretty gross."*

"That sounds cool," Matt continued. *"The highlight of my day was recess."*

"My math teacher, Mr. Burrows, is really nice. He seems to enjoy his job."

"So it sounds like everyone is having a good day, today," Jake said with a smile. *"I think I may have seen my future dream house today."*

"I bet it has a full basement, two-car garage, and five bedrooms," Alicia blurted.

"Yeah, and a place for a large flat screen TV," Matt added.

"Well, it sure has room enough," Jake continued. *"I did count five bedrooms."*

"Sure sounds like a dream to me, dear." Terry said with a wry smile. Her budgetary work certainly indicated that no such purchase would be in their immediate future plans.

"Remember Bob Peters at the constructions site, honey? His Aunt Bertha died and left him an old farmhouse with acres of land only about ten miles from here. He wants me to quote on some plumbing work on it. It's pretty run down as far as the plumbing goes, but the house looks really solid. Anyway, I could not help but think about how great it would be to have a place like that for this family. It has a huge barn as well."

"Wow, a barn," Matt said with a smile. *"My friend, Billy, used to talk about jumping into big piles of hay inside his grandparents barn. That sounds like fun."*

"Hold on, little guy. Remember I called it my dream house. So honey, how was your day?"

"I'll share with you later. Right now, who wants a brownie?"

Suddenly, the thought of brownies seemed to outweigh the need to have a conversation around the table. Terry desired to talk about the budget without the children present, so desert offered a convenient escape.

DENNIS A. MCINTYRE

Balancing the Budget

Somehow, Terry had managed to postpone talking about her day during the family time at the dinner table. As a rule, everyone shared, but the introduction of freshly baked brownies seemed to take on a higher priority. After the children were in bed, Terry placed the spreadsheet for bills and expenses on the dinning room table.

"I didn't get a chance to talk about my day, honey. Could you come to the table? I want to show you something."

"Can't you just tell me about your day? This easy chair sure feels good right now."

"You need to come here to actually see what I did today."

"Okay. You did make a wonderful meal, however."

"After you left this morning, I picked up my Bible and started reading. I opened it to the Book of Proverbs and began reading. I think God had a message for us."

"You got me curious." Jake kissed her on the back of her neck while looking over her shoulder at the spreadsheet opened on the table.

"The words talked about wisdom. I underlined the verses that seemed to leap out at me. Here Jake, read them."

"Okay." Jake read about ants, coneys (badgers), locusts, and lizards. *"Pretty strange creatures to associate them with wisdom?"*

"I thought so too, but then I began to dig a little deeper. When you left this morning, your thoughts were on having a bigger place to live. I wondered how we could afford another place and prayed about it. When I opened the Word of God, these were the words that I read. I felt that God was trying to tell me something."

"Maybe the farm I saw today had all of those critters," Jake chuckled.

"I want you to be serious with me. I think God wants us to be like the ants."

"We are. Six people in this small place seems to be pretty cramped. I think ants tend to pack themselves even tighter."

"Oh honey, that's not it at all. God is talking about the wisdom of ants. They gather food all summer, so they can survive a long winter."

"We have barely enough room to store what we have, let alone more."

"I think He wants us to learn how to save for the home we really want. Let me show you."

Terry began to show her husband the difference between needs and wants as she referred to the list. The monthly expenditures that were necessary included rent, utility payments, insurance, and vehicle payments.

"I took the time to go back twelve months to get an average cost for most of the items. Until the vehicles are paid for, we need $2756 per month to meet our current obligations.

"You forgot food. We do have to eat you know."

"You're right, but not the same as we have in the past. We have pizza at least once a week and often twice. The deliveryman gets about twenty-five dollars each time we order. The meal you just had, including the brownies, cost about ten dollars, and we have leftovers."

"It was delicious, dear."

"Better than pizza."

"Much better."

"Every time that you have a great week, you want to celebrate by taking all of us out for a lavish meal. We spend enough in that one dinner to pay for over a month of quality meals at home."

"But, honey, I love to take you guys out for a special time."

"We can have special times at home. Besides, would you rather eat out or have a bigger place to live? I am convinced that we can reach the goal of home ownership, if we follow the wisdom of the ants."

"Now you got me curious. You have been busy today, haven't you?"

"Remember when you wanted to buy that new truck for work. It was right after you landed a big job."

"I remember, honey. Paul told me I was nuts and didn't need the extra five years of payments."

"Paul was right. In eleven months we will have your truck paid for at the present rate. That reduces our month debt by $365, which could go towards saving for a house."

"I will still need new wheels someday. Besides, I get to write off that cost as a work expense."

"Still, when you need a vehicle, it does not have to be new."

"I guess we can trust God to provide, huh?"

"That's just it, honey. We need to have faith and not act on whims. I think He brought us together and wants the best for us, don't you?"

"He's the best thing that ever happened in my life. I owe my life to Him. Without Jesus, my life was lost and a mess."

"So, with Jesus, our lives are rich in blessings. I feel that way, too. I think God wants us to realize that we can have our dreams fulfilled if we persevere like those pesky little ants carrying loads of food away under the picnic table. They don't seem to stuff themselves for the moment. They have real purpose."

"Maybe you are right. We could be more frugal with what we have."

"If we had started cutting out the extras over the past twelve months, we would have enough in savings to pay off your truck. That would sure help with any possible mortgage application."

Jake looked at Terry's figures and began to soak the information in. He remembered his conversation with Paul over buying a new truck for work. He tried to justify to Paul that he could do so much more with the new wheels, but Paul convinced him otherwise. During the good times, Jake thought more about what he could do to better the lives of his family. Terry was showing him that a steadfast longer-term plan would bring about more lasting satisfaction. As a man, it was difficult to think that ants were smarter than he was, but they certainly were more diligent. Terry's work that day had a profound impact on Jake's mindset. The farmhouse and barn painted a picture in Jake's mind that he could not shake. The potential was there for great things. None of which were possible using any short-term financial whims. The lesson of the ants made sense.

Terry continued with the discussion for some time. She talked about the small salamander (newt) that perched itself on the window ledge and seemed to nod with approval. Jake was moved to pray with Terry over their finances. The moment was complete for Terry as well. She wondered how well her husband would take her plan to conserve, and was genuinely surprised by his reaction. Terry thought about the old sewing machine in the closet as a vehicle to save money by making outfits for the kids, or to make Christmas presents. A yard sale or two might become a possibility. She was content with the life she had, but longed for Jake's dreams as a provider to become reality as well.

THE ESTIMATE

Before going to bed, Jake began to make a sketch of each room in the farmhouse that needed plumbing work, starting with the kitchen. He had made some notes during the tour of the house with a few added details. As he completed each phase, he could not get away from the thought that it could be a great place to raise his family. Bob discussed selling it, but Jake was in no position to make an offer. Yet, he began to place a dishwasher and double bowl sink precisely where it would go if the house was his.

The development still had plenty of work for the next eight to ten weeks, so anything additional could be considered a bonus. Bob was not in any hurry to get started, but Jake thought about working a few extra evenings and Saturdays. During the evening times he thought the kids would enjoy taking the trip with him. They sure sounded enthusiastic when Jake mentioned the hayloft in the barn. Still, he didn't want to get their hopes up. The next day he presented a rough draft of the estimate to Bob for consideration. If his figures were too far out of line, then he could make some adjustments. Approaching the estimate as if it was his own may have included a few, somewhat extravagant extras.

"Hey, Bob. Got a minute?"
"Sure, Jake. What's up?"

"I put together a quick estimate of your property's plumbing work. Take a look."

"I'll say that was quick. What did you do, stay up all night?"

"I had all the information in my head and wanted to get it down on paper. Remember, it's a rough draft. There's room for negotiation."

"Let me take it with me. I'll take a look at it before lunch. We can discuss the details then. Okay with you, Jake?"

"Sure thing. I got work to do anyway."

Bob folded he papers in half and stuffed them in his jacket pocket. As he left, Jake wondered if he should have said more about the estimate. Replacing all of the large black iron drains throughout the house was a major undertaking with a high price tag. He wondered if that would scare Bob into getting another estimate. Still, he thought that it was a more than fair price. But, would someone else only quote the bare minimum and make a lower offer to perform the work. These and other questions nagged at Jake all morning. By the time the noon whistle blew, Jake had taken on enough anxiety to last a month.

"Hey, Jake. How 'bout a burger, on me."

"You bought last time. This one is on me." Then he pulled out his wallet, which had only a few dollars. *"I need to stop at an ATM first, however."*

"No need. You can pay another day. Besides, I am excited with your estimate. Are you sure you haven't sold yourself short? It looks really good to me."

Somehow, those words gripped Jake's heart. He had worked himself up with worry and doubt for no reason. Jake's heart went from racing with anticipation to only a murmur. It was as if God was tugging on him to just have more faith and trust Him. The moment was one that Jake would recall several times that afternoon.

"So Bob, do you have any questions about the work?

"I don't see any fixtures quoted, just the labor and materials to install them. Any recommendations there?"

"Well, I was thinking about a brushed brass or stainless look throughout for faucets."

"I like both, Jake."

"You need to replace the kitchen countertop. Depending on what you chose, will affect the choice of sink. You could go with a double-bowl stainless look. It's pretty common."

"What would you like to see? I trust your insights. Besides, I have never been good at home decor. Just ask my wife," Bob said with a wry smile.

"I would love to see a granite countertop with a stainless double-bowl sink, the kind with a narrow side for food preparation and a large deep side for washing. The granite would really set the kitchen off. Its large enough to add an island to match in the future."

"My brother-in-law has something like that in his house. It does make a huge difference."

"You can get the granite installed for less than fifty dollars a square foot with the economy down as it is. There are some real deals out there."

"You show three full baths as well."

"I thought you had too many rooms in that house for the one and a half bathrooms there. My thoughts were along the lines of who would want to live there."

"Okay. Where do you see my best client base coming from?"

"Traditional farms attract large families. People move there to get away from city life, raise a family, and run their own business. Its tough work, but, for those people, very rewarding. I split the rooms upstairs to allow two or three rooms to share a bathroom. You could even make one room into a master bedroom-bath combination. The cost to complete the drains and water lines would not be very much, *if done at the same time. To upgrade later would cost considerably more."*

"I suppose, I could turn it into some kind of bed and breakfast place if I made it a four-bath house."

"You could at that. Although, I don't know how many people would want a view of a barn."

"Still, I like the idea of one bedroom with its own bath. Add that to your estimate."

"I will. Did you see the line item about replacing all of the black iron? Are you good with that?"

"Not only good, but that pipe has to go. I cleaned out a four-inch drain line for my aunt several years ago. What a mess. Today's plastic is so much better."

"You bet. I still need to talk to the county about the well and you might want to have someone examine the leech field. There is a development about a mile away with sewer lines. If the county has any plans to pass by your property, you can save a bundle, and I can include a garbage disposal unit in the kitchen."

"I will check that out. I have a good friend on the board. If they have such plans, he will know."

"Well, Jake. I am impressed. Finish the estimate with the extras we discussed and get back to me. I told you that I am not good with decorating, so pick out what you would select if it were your house. I trust your judgments."

"I'll try and get you the best rates. Sometimes, my distributors offer some great deals on stocked items."

"I believe in you Jake. We will talk later."

The two men completed their lunch and parted company. Jake could not believe what just transpired. He entered the meeting with great anxiety and left feeling at peace. Bob's words were uplifting, encouraging, and extremely comforting, especially, when it came to selecting items based on if the house were Jake's. Bob did not know that was, exactly, what he did the night before.

THE DINNER TABLE

J ake seemed to be on fire the rest of the day. The conversation with Bob about the farmhouse work seemed to release extra adrenalin, as he completed even more work then he had planned for the day at the construction site. He would normally start closing things up shortly after five to ensure that he would be home by six. Bob saw Jake's truck still at the site at five-forty and went to find him.

"Jake. Jake, are you in there?"

"I'm here, Bob."

"Do you know what time it is? You are normally gone by now."

"Oh my gosh. I guess I got carried away today. I'm closing up. Thanks for letting me know."

"You're welcome. You must have a lot on your mind today. One of my workers said he heard you singing so it must have been good stuff."

"Singin. I don't sing."

"Yeah, well, he said that too. Anyway, don't leave that pretty little wife of yours waiting, Jake. Work can wait another day."

"I'm right behind you. Thanks again."

Jake proceeded to pack up his toolbox and threw it into the back of his truck. He arrived home about fifteen minutes later than usual, but no one seemed to notice. Jake always tried to make a clean break from work by the time he came home, but had not fully prepared himself today. The discussion about the farmhouse with Bob was still heavy on his mind.

"Sorry I'm late, honey." Jake gave Terry a warm embrace as the aroma of the kitchen tantalized his senses.

"You're not late, dinner won't be ready for another ten or fifteen minutes. I must have put too many things in the oven at the same time. How was your day?"

"Fantastic! I was a bit apprehensive about the estimate that I gave Bob this morning, but he loved it. He even wants me to help pick out fixtures as if it was my own."

"I have not seen you this excited, since our wedding night."

"There's something about this work that is so encouraging. I think God has some part of it. I want you and the kids to come with me tonight and see the farm."

"I think the children would love that, especially Matthew. He has been talking about jumping off a hayloft all afternoon, since he came home from school."

Jake glanced towards the living room at Matt, who was playing a board game with his sisters on the floor.

"Hey, kids. What game are you playing?"

"Sorry, dad."

"I didn't mean that I wanted to join you. I just wanted to start a conversation."

"No, dad. The name of the game is 'Sorry.' Haven't you ever played it?"

"No, I haven't. I never really played very many board games. When I was with my friends we played Atari or war games outside."

"Atari? What's that?"

"It's like a two-dimensional version of your video games. Anyway, I was wondering if you guys would like to take a ride to see the farm after dinner."

Matt leaped to his feet with a loud *"You bet."*

"Whoa, fella. I said, after dinner."

"Mom, how soon are we eatin?"

The girls also approved of the idea, but with a bit less emotion. Jake went into the living room to watch the kids complete their game

"So what's the object here?"

Alicia pointed out that each player had four pieces of the same color, and they all started in the 'Home' circle of that color. The board had the colors pretty scattered around, so Nicole described how they moved by the total of two dice. Diana interrupted, to describe how a move could send someone else back to the color's home space to start all over again. Then Matt described the object was to be the first to get all one's color into the tower's circle.

By the time the game was completed, supper was ready. Terry smiled as she overheard the children try to teach the game to their father. It was a moment of reflection on just how far they had come as a family.

"Dinner's ready. Come and eat."

Matt rushed to the table and sat down.

"That was quick young man. Now go wash your hands. You have been playing on the floor."

The bathroom had a line as all four kids washed up. Jake stared for a moment and reflected about the farmhouse.

"Terry, honey. See that. Bob and I discussed the three bath proposal for this house and added a fourth as a master bedroom bath combination. We have two baths here and the kids share one of them.

I know the farmhouse is not ours, but wouldn't it be wonderful if they had separate baths?"

"It would, dear, it would. But, we need to live in the present right now."

"We can still have our dreams, can't we?"

"That we can. God has brought us so far together. We can trust Him to bring us further."

The dinner table had mashed potatoes, biscuits, chicken gravy, corn, green beans, and baked chicken. While Jake admired the food, the rest of the family took their seats.

"Who wants to pray tonight?" Terry asked.

"I will." Matt blurted. He seemed to be in quite a hurry to start eating. *"Dear God. Bless this great food and let us enjoy our visit to the farm tonight. Amen."*

"That was quick, Matt," Jake inserted. *But, I guess it covers the bases. Dig in."*

The usual conversation at the dinner table was pretty limited. Mashed potatoes and gravy was a special treat, and each child enjoyed seconds. Matt seemed to be putting out some sort of fire in his belly.

"You need to slow down young man or you'll get an upset stomach. That wouldn't be very good if you plan on jumping into a pile of hay."

Matt smiled and heeded the advice.

"So, Diana, how's your friend, Steven, doing?" Jake asked.

"Fine." Diana responded with a snap.

"That did not sound very encouraging." Terry added.

"We hardly talked at all today. Belinda saw to that."

"Okay. Who is Belinda?"

"She sits next to him in class. She's such a flirt."

"Steven is just trying to be friends with people. You did say he was new to the area. Let him make friends and don't be so judgmental, young lady."

"You're probably right, mom. But I really looked forward to spending time with Steven after yesterday."

"Give it time. I'm sure things will work out between you. You may even make a new friend with Belinda."

"Dissect any more frogs today, Matt?" Jake inquired.

"No, but I did get an 'A' on the project."

"That's wonderful, son." Jake responded. *"I can't remember ever getting a grade as high as a 'B', let alone an 'A,'"*

"You must have, dad," Nicole chimed in. *"You're one of the smartest people I know."*

"I'll second that," Alicia added.

The dynamics of the discussion around the table had a profound impact on both Terry and Jake. When Jake was each child's age, he was already heavily involved with drugs, alcohol and gangs. His stepfather barked more orders than he openly shared from his heart. His mother only spoke when asked. The conversation around the dinner table was totally opposite from anything Jake had known in his childhood. Terry's abusing husband left little room for any quality discussions a s well. She spent her time trying to console Diana and Matt was just a toddler when they divorced, Still, the discussions brought joy and a lot of satisfaction to everyone.

Terry thought that she had made plenty of food to have leftovers the next day. Except for a few biscuits and two pieces of chicken, the food had been devoured.

"Great meal, mom." Matt yelled.

"Yeah, mom. You sure are a great cook," the rest added.

"Now can we go see the farm, dad? ' Matt said with a huge smile on his face.

"As soon as everyone helps pick up their dishes and cleans the table, we can go.'

Terry stared at Jake with a look of amazement. The idea of looking at someplace new took on a measure of excitement for each child. The table was cleared, the dishwasher was loaded, and the kitchen was cleaned in record time. They also noticed that the children did not have their usual barrage of 'who's doing what' the children realized that comments. They actually worked in harmony together. Somehow, they realized that as soon as the kitchen was clean, they could go visit the farm. They worked with a purpose. Jake and Terry were enamored by the moment.

"I guess we better not disappoint them," Jake said as he winked at Terry.

THE VISIT

Terry's eight-year old van may have had a lot of miles, but at least it was paid for. Loading everybody in it was a snap compared to Jake's truck with the extended cab, which was filled with work clothes and other materials. Terry often referred to her vehicle as a bus to haul the kids around to their various activities. Having everyone together for a ride was usually reserved for Sundays and an occasional vacation.

"Everyone buckled up?" Jake shouted.

"We're good back here," Alicia responded. *"How far did you say it was?"*

"It's rally close. I'd say about eight or nine miles."

"It's hard to believe that there is a farm so close," Diana responded. *"All I have seen around here are houses and more houses."*

"Florida may be known for oranges, beaches, and sunshine, but it is the second or third largest state for raising cattle. Many people don't know that. Keep your eyes open and you may see what I mean," Jake answered.

As they rode, Jake pointed out places when farming and orange groves had been replaced with large housing developments.

"I guess we can be thankful for those housing areas, as they keep your father in business."

"There's some cows up ahead," Matt shouted. *"Is that where the farm is?"*

"Not yet, son. Keep looking as it is not much farther."

A few minutes later, Jake pulled off the road onto a stony path. He remembered a locked gate and, for a moment, wondered if they would even get in. Bob had the key to unlock it, but Jake forgot to ask if he could borrow it that evening. The thoughts were short-lived as the gate was already open. Upon arriving at the farmhouse, Jake noticed Bob's truck parked near the barn. He told his family to wait in the car until he got the okay from Bob. In all that excitement, Jake did not clear everything with the farm's owner. Without approval he could be considered as trespassing. As he walked towards the barn, the thought of having to get a key to get into the house seemed like a dumb oversight on his part. It was not his house, though he spent much of that day thinking about the possibility. Reality seemed to sink in as he thought about his oversight regarding the keys.

"Bob. Bob are you in here?"

The barn door was open and Jake heard Bob respond,

"Over here, Jake."

"Sorry to come in unannounced, but I wanted to get a few more measurements. My family is here as well."

"Tell them to come on in. The house is open, Jake. Give them a grand tour."

"Thanks, Bob." Jake went outside the barn and motioned his family to join him. *"I didn't know if I could even get onto the property, as I forgot to ask you for some keys."*

"Come anytime, Jake. I made an extra set of keys for you. The small one, here, is for the gate. This one with the double edge is for

the barn doors, and the other one is for the house. Keep them in your truck. You will need them when you start the work."

"I guess that means that you want me to perform the work. I haven't completed the final work for you."

"I trust you, Jake. You are a man of character and honesty. Besides, I see you daily. If you mess with me, I know where you live," Bob said with a smile.

A few moments later, Terry and the kids stood at the front of the barn.

"Hi Mr Peters," Terry shouted.

"Hi Terry, but first call me, Bob. What a fine group of children you have there. I'm working on the old tractor in the back of the barn. Send the kids to me and go take a tour with your husband."

Without hesitation, the children's curiosity cause them to run to the back of the barn, while Terry joined her husband to look at the house. They walked the weed-ridden stony path to the rear door, while Jake pointed out where the well was located. They entered the storage room, which still held the clutter. Then the door to the kitchen area was opened and Jake could not wait to show Terry his plans.

Remember, honey, this is not our house."

"I know, but Bob insisted that I treat it as if it was. Besides, dreams can be good, can't they?"

"They can, as long you realize they are dreams. This sure is a big room for a kitchen."

"Farmers loved to eat. Anyway, this is what I drew up for renovation. You will have to use your imagination, as much of what you see will have to go."

"I don't want to interfere with your business, but I can already see a few changes," Terry said as she squeezed Jake's hand.

"Like what?"

First, the double-bowl sink needs to be centered under this window. I do much of my work here and need to have a good view of the kids or visitors. Does that make sense?"

"I confess. I didn't think of that." Jake took out a red-leaded pencil and began sketching the change. *"So where do you envision the dishwasher and stove going, honey?'*

"My first thoughts would be here and there," she said as she made additional red marks on his sketch.

"You said 'first thoughts.' What was your second?"

"The room is so big, that it could use an island. The stove could be part of the island, with the dishwasher here, near the sink. I could almost reach everything, including the 'fridge' by standing between the island and the sink."

"Now who's doing the dreaming?" Jake said as he caressed his wife's hand. *"I had the same thoughts about an island. I will make two different sketches, one with and one without it."*

"I love these old cupboards. They need a little restoration, but they would go well with some old style fixtures.

"I suggested the brush-stainless or brass look to Bob. What do you think?"

"The brush-stainless is good, but in a faucet with the tall neck. Bob may want to replace the lighting fixtures with a similar look. The cupboards could have brush-stainless handles and hinges to match."

"I see what you mean, at least I think I do. You can show me sometime, when we look at fixtures together. Bob wants me to do that as well. I'm sure he wouldn't mind a woman's touch, especially here in the kitchen."

"I suggested granite. It comes in a wide range of colors, patterns, and is durable."

"Granite will do very nicely. The cabinets can be sanded and painted with colors to match. I think a medium or dark color choice for granite would draw the room a bit closer and warmer."

"Good idea. I will pass that on as well. Let me take you through the rest of the house."

Jake began walking through the dining room and then over to the downstairs half-bath. Terry stopped to admire the spacious dining area, large wood moldings, and decoratively carved features.

"Sure is beautiful, honey. I just love the moldings. You just don't see wood carved like that in newer homes. It's beautiful."

"Those old farmers were also fine craftsmen, huh?"

"They sure were. It would be a shame to not maintain as much of this look as possible. This room can feed our family, even if everyone brought friends."

"I had that same feeling. Take a look at this bathroom. I want to move this wall back to add a tub and shower combination."

"I can picture one of these old-fashioned wrought-iron tubs. Do they still make them?"

"I'm sure they can be found. Anyway, this room could be a good bedroom or den with a bathroom."

That would be a good use of the space. I guess with that in mind, a shower would work."

"Makes sense. I'll modify my sketch. Now come on upstairs."

The solid wood stairs also captured Terry's imagination. There were four steps to the first landing, eight to the next, and four more to a large open space. Looking up at the stairs from the front room was something like a scene from "Gone With The Wind." The lofty ceiling and intricate wood curved moldings seemed elegant, despite their dull luster due to wear. Nevertheless, as she walked up the stairs, she hardly heard a creak sound. The structure was solid.

The upper level left another moment of reflection. The cherry-planked flooring seemed to go on forever in all directions. Each doorway had a similar decorative pattern of moldings, like the dining room below. Each door seemed much thicker than those in the apartments. Jake motioned for Terry to come over to the one bathroom, located near the top of the stairs. It was somewhat central to the five large rooms.

I plan on adding a bathroom here." Jake motioned with his hands so Terry would understand. *"This bath can serve this end of the house. The two rooms facing the front of the house could be separated by a bath."*

"That would work."

"The last room would be a long way from the existing bathroom, so I suggested a master-bedroom-bath combination for that room. The rooms on each side of the old bathroom could share it. Anyway, Bob wants me to quote a fourth bathroom."

"Wow! This room is huge."

"Can you picture this end as a completed bath, and over here a larger walk-in closet?"

"There sure is enough space. This house is huge. It doesn't look it from the outside."

I think the house started out small and grew as the family grew. They kept pushing out walls and built rooms upstairs. That's why the kitchen is so big. I suspect that it was a storage area onetime, like the first rooms we came into."

"Just think what it would have looked like if they had a dozen kids."

Both Jake and Terry laughed and hugged each other. Jake added more of Terry's suggestions to his sketch and the two went out to check on the kids.

"I hope our children are not being a bother to Mr. Peters," Terry said as the two left the farmhouse.

"They must be occupied. We have not seen them come into the hose."

"Matt, Diana, Alicia and Nicole! Where are you?" Jake yelled.

"We're all up here. Mr. Peters moved some straw into a huge pile and we are jumping into it from above. Watch me dad."

As soon as Matt said that, he leaped from a height of about ten feet into the pile. Then he slid down another four or five feet to the loft's floor. You would have thought they were all youngsters visiting Disney World for the first time. It was obvious that were enjoying themselves, immensely.

"Where's Mr. Peters?"

"Over here, Jake. I just got this International Harvester tractor ready for a test spin. It needs a good coat of new red paint, but it runs like a champ."

"Fire it up, Bob. I'd like to hear how she sounds."

"How do you know it's a she?"

"Don't we men refer to our toys as 'she? Check out the names on the boats at a marina, sometime."

"I get your point. Here goes nothing.

The old tractor sputtered for a moment and seemed to run rough. Bob played with the choke a bit until it had a smooth idle. The sound was still quite loud, as the rising exhaust pipe shook against the tractor's frame. Bob stepped on the gas and the noise seemed to have a welcomed resonance to it.

"It's music to my ears, Jake. I just love the sound of a tractor."

"I hear you. I think it sounds more like a 'He."

"Not when I first fire her up. You have to caress her a bit to get her calmed down."

"I'll remember you said that, when I see your wife." Jake snickered.

"Help me hook up the wagon. I think these kids would like a hayride."

The two men hauled an old wagon from the backside of the barn. It had several bales of straw loaded on it's flat bed. The dual axle looked like something from an old truck, with white-wall tires from the sixties. Still, the tires had enough are to hold four kids.

With his family aboard, Jake hopped on the back of the tractor. He was interested in watching Bob run through the gear shifting and barking operations. The experience was a new one for Jake as well. The ride took about ten minutes and covered a little more than a mile. Bob pointed out some historical facts about the property as they rode.

The farmhouse and barn were on the north end of the property. Jake pointed out the new housing development a bit further north as they passed the first gate.

"Over there, Bob. That's where the new public sewer lines are being run. If we connect with the, it would sure save a lot of work and trouble"

"I put a call into my friend on the board about it. I should hear from him by the end of the week."

"Rides over. Did everyone have a good time?"

"Oh, yeah" was the enthusiastic response.

"I will pull the tractor and trailer into the barn. No need to unhook it now. Did you get everything you needed?"

"I think so. Terry has added her input as well, which I think you will like."

"Great! I look forward to your estimate and plans. See you tomorrow."

"Thanks for everything, Bob." Each member of the family added their thanks as well.

The drive home for Jake was filled with joy as well. Matt asked when they would come back again.

THE APPLIANCE STORE

The Wilson clan was still buzzing about the evening's experience as they returned to their apartment.

"Sounds like everyone had a great time tonight," Jake inserted.

"When can we go again?" Matt added.

"Your dad will be doing some work there over the next few weeks, so you'll get another opportunity to visit."

"More like a couple of months," Jake inserted. *"Bob needs to get the zoning board's input about the sewer lines, which could take awhile. I can only work weekends and evenings as well, so you kids should have several opportunities to come with me."*

"We sure had fun playing in the hay loft," each child uttered, almost in unison.

"I think Bob had fun watching you as well."

"Still, your mom and I don't want you to get your hopes too high. Once the work is done, we can only visit by invitation."

"That's okay, dad. But, we sure had a great time tonight."

"Speaking of the time, it's late. You guys need to brush your teeth and get to bed. Tomorrow is a school day.

Terry followed the children to their rooms to pray with them, while Jake went to the kitchen to work on estimates. He decided to redraw the kitchen's layout, due to the clutter of red line modifications from the visit. As he placed a six-foot long island opposite the sink, the possibilities began to come alive. Soon, it grew to eight feet with a wrap around countertop extension for stool seating and several storage cabinets below. By the time Terry returned, Jake had a detailed view almost completed.

"What do you think, honey? The kids could have breakfast on the backside of the island."

"Jake, it's not our house."

"I know, but Bob wanted me to designs if it was."

"Why do you think he did that?'

"I think he wants to attract a large family. We do have six in ours."

"I guess if you make it appeal to us, other families would also find it attractive. The extra wide island is a nice touch as well. It makes the room look smaller and cozier."

"I placed the dishwasher here," Jake pointed to the sketch. *"The door opens to one side of the sink, so you can rinse and place dishes all in one motion."*

"I can picture the motion is from left to right or clockwise for me, being right-handed. Your placement works well for me, but is opposite for a left-handed person.

"Good point. I will pass that on to Bob for consideration. Anyway, that decision does not need to be made until installation time."

"Where do you see the stove and 'fridge' going?"

"I was thinking about having the far wall for the refrigerator, with the stove near the sin. Where it is now."

Terry began to walk through the process of preparing a meal in her mind. He idea of having each appliance conveniently located around her work area made sense. Every detail was carefully considered for optimum space usage. If the children were to eat at the counter, then the door to the refrigerator needed to be easily accessible as well.

"Terry, do you know what time it is?"

"Nearly midnight," she said with a startled look as she glanced at the clock.

They looked at each other in amazement. That day had been one, which would stay in their memory for a long time. The old farmhouse was not theirs, but it drew them together as a family. It showed them that if they focused on something worthwhile together, everything else seemed trivial. Terry remembered the lesson of the ants gathering food for a long winter.

"Jake, honey. I think God wants for us to work on a goal together. Today was truly a blessing, but I think He wants to bless us even more."

"Today was special, wasn't it? I have never seen the kids so happy, just being together."

"God used a farmhouse to show us the simple pleasures in life can be the most meaningful."

"Yeah! No video games or computers. They just had good old-fashioned fun together. God is so good. We are truly blessed."

Before retiring, Jake and Terry prayed together, as they usually did, but this time with more specifics. Jake thanked God for Bob, the additional work, and the great family they shared together that evening. Terry asked for wisdom and insights, so she would know God's will for her life. She longed for the deeper meaning in the wisdom of the parable she read about the ants, the locusts and the lizards. Somehow, she felt that God was speaking directly to her through those words. As Jake listened, he felt led to pray for that same wisdom as well.

The next day, Jake presented his drawing to Bob with the associated costs. Jake tried to explain why the appliances had been placed as they were, based on Terry's discussion, but Bob was quick to recognize the logic.

"*I couldn't have done it better myself, Jake. I can see a large family using the kitchen as a gathering place. Tell Terry that she did a great job.*" Bob said that with a smirk, as he could see a woman's touch in the layout.

"*I will. I will complete the bedrooms tonight.*"

"*You do that, but make sure the wife of yours has her say.*" Bob said once again with a smile.

"*I will. I want to thank you for entertaining my children last night. They had a blast.*"

"*My pleasure. I think I had as much fun or even more. It brought out my childhood. That old farm has fond memories for me.*"

"*You were like a kid on the tractor.*"

"*I drove that thing when I was matt's age. Next time you're out, I need to let him have a go behind the wheel.*"

"*That would truly make his day.*"

"*So, Jake. What are you doing for lunch today?*"

"*I have no plans at the moment. Why?*"

"*You have got me interested in checking out appliances. Want to join me?*"

"*Only, if you let me buy the burgers.*"

"*You got it. I will pick you up a t noon.*"

The whistle blew, and Bob was right on time.

"*Jake, have you been to that new discount appliance store that just opened near here?*"

"*Not yet.*"

"*I have a nephew working there. He just finished high school. I Think I will give him some business, if he is in today.*"

"*Sounds good, but don't forget the burgers. What's your nephew's name?*"

"*I just call him 'BJ,' like the Bandit film. Anyway, he might help me get a good deal and earn something for college in the process.*"

Bob pulled into a drive-thru at a fast food chain to get lunch and then headed to the store. They barely had enough time to gulp down the food, when they arrived. Upon entering the store, Jake pointed to a sign over the appliance section, and they headed over. Bob spotted his nephew and called out to him.

"Bee jay."

"Hi Uncle Bob."

"This is my friend, Jake. I need to look at new appliances for the kitchen at the farm."

"Aunt Bertha's?"

"Yeah! Jake is going to do some plumbing work for me, and the old stuff has to go. Can you make me a good deal? I need a stove, 'fridge', and dishwasher to start."

"I'll do the best I can, Uncle Bob. Let's start with the refrigerator. What do you have in mind?'

"I was thinking about a side by side unit in brushed-stainless. What do you think, Jake?"

"There's plenty of room for a side-by-side 'fridge', and the brushed-stainless will go well with the fixtures."

As Jake spoke, his eyes seemed to be focused on the store clerk. There was something familiar in BJ's eyes, as if he had seen him somewhere before. The name on his shirt said "B.J. Gates," which did nothing to clear up his wonderment. BJ was a good looking, dark haired, clean cut teenager and very respectful, especially towards his uncle. Still, Jake could not shake the feeling that he knew the young man.

BJ made printouts of each appliance selected and went to the office to discuss a lumped together deal with his boss. He returned a few minutes later with a price and presented it to his uncle.

This is a great price, BJ. Are you sure you are going to make something on the deal?"

"Don't worry, Uncle Bob. I'll do just fine."

"It's a deal then. Could you have the stuff delivered sometime next week? I will leave the address. You should come out and see the farm sometime as well."

"Next week should not be a problem, and I would love to see the farm. Do you have the old tractor running?"

He does." Jake inserted. *"We took a hayride with it last night."*

"Did Uncle Bob open her up? It can really fly in fourth gear."

"She needs a few gaskets replaced, but there's still a lot of fire in the old belly, BJ." Bob insisted.

"Let me know when the delivery is scheduled, BJ. Jake or I will be there to open the gate."

"How does next Friday afternoon sound, say between two and four?"

"Works for me. Come on Jake. Lets get back to work so I can pay for this stuff."

The ride back to the work site initiated a new discussion.

"There is something about BJ that makes me think I know him from someplace, Bob."

"He's a special young man. He has had a rough life."

"He sure looks like he has come through it well."

"He had to mature early. He never got to know his father, and his mother was in a new relationship almost monthly."

"I guess I can, somewhat, relate to that. My dad left when I was five, but mom remarried a year or so later. They have been together ever since. I learned to love my stepfather, so I cannot imagine what BJ went through without a father."

"BJ's mother died when he turned sixteen. Aunt Bertha was like a mother to him, even when his mom was alive."

"Perhaps, God has something extra special for BJ, by letting him go through all of that."

"Perhaps, Jake, perhaps. God can direct our paths in wonderful ways my friend."

"He sure can. I am living proof of that "

HOMEMADE SOUP

The smell of good home cooking was evident as Jake came home. Jake was able to complete more work than he planned for the day. The normal anxieties from work were gone, making the smell of something cooking in the kitchen very pleasing to Jake's senses.

"How was your day, honey?"

"It was great. Bob and I went to pick out appliances overcome. Supper sure smells good.

"I have a large kettle of homemade vegetable soup and some biscuits ready."

Jake went to take a quick shower and change clothes. The aroma seemed to draw him to the table much quicker than usual.

"That was quick, honey. Dinner is served."

"Is this a first, dear?"

"What do you mean?"

"I don't remember having homemade soup before, at least not made by you."

"I had a lot of small leftover vegetables and potatoes to use up and thought I would give it a try. Besides, we should have plenty for

leftovers. The canned soups still leave us hungry later. We always wish we had more during the meal."

"This soup is terrific."

"Yeah, mom. You rock." Matt added.

Each child shared something about his or her day during the meal. Matt's latest science project received an 'A.' Nicole and Alicia Shared their experience on the farm with all their friends, who expressed some for of jealousy. Diana made a new friend during lunchtime.

"So how was your day, Terry?"

"Making soup consumed a lot of it, but the experience was wonderful. I felt peaceful, as if God was right there helping me slice carrots or peel potatoes."

"You did ask for wisdom last night. Now you know how to make great soup."

"I also asked for direction for my/our life. I was able to focus on one thing today, namely, making soup, and everything went very well. I should be tired, but I feel a bit rejuvenated. What happened in your day, Jake?"

"I met a young man at the appliance store. He goes by the name 'BJ' and is Bob's nephew. There was something about him that seemed so familiar. I could not put my finger on what it was, but he was on my mind ever since."

"Perhaps, God has placed him in your life for a purpose."

"I thought about that all day, honey. I am just not sure about what that purpose is. It might just be a coincidence or something."

"If that young man is on your mind and heart, then it is no coincidence. God will reveal His plan at some point."

"I believe that too. Anyway, we might see BJ from time to time on the farm."

"What do you mean?"

"He lost his mother a couple years ago, and Bob's Aunt Bertha took him in until he died. He never knew his father, who left after he was born."

"That sounds like you. Your son, from your first marriage, never knew you, right?"

"Maybe that's the connection, although I don't know how I might feel, as I did by just the initial eye contact with BJ. All I remember from my son was his name, "Brandon."

"I'm sure, that if there is a connection, God will fill in the gaps over time."

"No doubt He will. Anyway, Bob bought the kitchen appliances, which gets delivered next Friday."

"That was pretty quick, honey."

"Yeah! I only gave him the sketch this morning. By the way, Bob wanted you to know that he really appreciated your input in the layout."

"Tell Bob it was my pleasure, It was also fun."

"I will tell him, but I think he already knew about the fun part."

Jake spent a couple hours enjoying spending time with the kids before working to complete the bathroom layouts. The next day, he discussed the details with Bob.

"As I expected, Jake, these look great. Now tell me what you need to get started."

"I can run the new drain lines and copper, regardless of whether we have to stay on the septic system or can connect to the public sewer lines. I can rough in everything."

"How much will the material costs be, give or take a thousand?"

"It shouldn't cost thousands, Bob, at least not until you add the fixture costs. A thousand, fifteen hundred tops, should cover the rough in materials."

"I will set up a twenty-five hundred dollar line of credit in your name with my supplier. They handle about everything. Let me know if

there is something you need that they don't have. They give me good rates on most items."

"I will talk to them tonight. I am ahead with my work, so I can close up early this afternoon and stop in. Your supplier is right on my way home, anyway."

"Take your wife with you sometime as well Have he look at the fixtures."

"In that case, maybe she can meet me there during lunch. She can bring a warmed bowl of that homemade soup we had last night."

"Homemade soup? She is going to spoil you. There is nothing better that homemade soup. I think it is the love that is added."

"Maybe that's it. Even the kids had seconds."

"Take my word from experience. It's the added love. Aunt Bertha made a lot of homemade soup during her life, and we felt special dining with her."

"You sure seem anxious to see the old place fixed up."

"Speaking of that, do you plan on working there on Saturday?"

"I guess, if the materials are on hand. I can start then. Why do you ask?"

"First, because I want to take that tractor and wagon out for a good workout, and I would love to let your kids help."

"I am sure they will be excited to hear that and delighted to test the wagon."

"Great! Second, I told BJ that if he needed some extra cash, then he could help restore the old cabinets in the kitchen. He's pretty good with carpentry work and enjoys it. Anyway, he said he could start on Saturday."

"I have done quite a bit of woodworking myself. So, even if the materials are not in, I could help BJ."

"Okay. Great. I'll see you there."

Something about this Saturday seemed to be uplifting for Bob. Jake could see it in his face. The thought of asking Matt if he would like to go on a hayride also brought a smile to Jake's face, not to mention the rest of the girls. Jake also thought about working with BJ. There was still something about that young man that pricked Jake's heart.

Jake gave Terry a call to see if she would meet him over lunch. The children were all in school, so she drove to Jake's work site with a freshly warmed bowl of soup. Then they went together to the supply house where Jake directed her to the kitchen and bath fixture sections for recommendations. Bob was especially interested in he insights. Jake proceeded to the counter to order the other materials and introduce himself.

"Mr. Wilson. We have about half the materials you need here at the warehouse. WE had a run on the four inch PVC piping this week, and our next shipment should be here next Thursday."

"That's okay. Can you hold everything until the pipe arrives? I can pick it up one load at a time."

"We can, but your order exceeds our minimum for free delivery. Would you like it dropped off at the site?"

"If you can do that, it would be wonderful. Let me write down the address."

"I know that place. Bob has supplies dropped there from time to time as well. Does he still keep the gate locked?"

"He does, but I have a key. Call me on my cell when you are ready to make the delivery, and I will meet you there."

Jake proceeded to write his phone number on the order. Then he went to find Terry.

"This place is great, honey. They even deliver."

"What do you think about this faucet, honey? It has the tall neck, but it also extends as a sprayer."

"That should work quite well in front of the kitchen window."

"I thought so, too, along with this soap dispenser. The two separate baths upstairs could use these faucets over here." Terry led Jake to the selection.

"I like your choices, honey. The downstairs could use the same one as well, don't you think?"

"It could, but I thought I thought this would work there. The ceilings downstairs are higher, so I thought a tall curved look might be nicer there."

"I never thought about that. I guess that;s why Bob wanted you to pick out that stuff, huh?"

"Women like to decorate. We just know what we like."

"We like to pick out tools," Jake said with a sheepish grin.

"I think the upstairs can have a more modern flair, but we should maintain the natural more rustic look for the downstairs. I saw an old-fashion tub with a shower attachment to match the sink's faucet over here. That should look nice downstairs, don't you think?"

"I see your point, honey. I will write these things down for Bob. What did you have in mind for the master bedroom faucet?"

"I was thinking that it should have a bit more elegance than the other baths. What do you think about a walk-in shower separate from the tub?"

"That works. I prefer to take showers anyway."

"The tub could be different from the standard rectangular ones, like that garden tub over there."

"I'll add that to the list for Bob as well." Jake pulled a flier from the wall holder to get the dimensions.

A few other items were measured as well, like the vanity possibilities, and they left. Looking at new fixtures was a unique experience for both Jake and Terry. Though it was for someone else, they enjoyed the time together. Perhaps, someday, they would have another opportunity to make similar choices together for a home of their own.

"I had a lot of fun today," Terry shared.

"Me , too, honey. I learned a lot."

"Like what?"

"Like what a great homemaker and interior decorator you are, dear."

"I learned something as well, Jake Wilson."

"I'll bite."

"You're trainable."

With that, they warmly hugged.

DENNIS A. MCINTYRE

THE CABINETS

The rest of the week seemed to pass quickly. Jake added some final touches to each bath, based on the additional measurements he had taken. Bob was pleased with the details and the price of the installation. Suddenly, Saturday had arrived. The children were up at the crack of dawn, anticipating the trip to the farm with dad. Jake promised to help BJ with the cabinetwork, and his plumbing materials would not be delivered until later that week.

"Wow! You kids are up early."

"Today is the day that you said we could go with you to the farm," Nicole blurted.

"You guys don't forget a thing."

"So, when are we leaving?"

"It's not even eight o'clock yet. Let's have breakfast. Then we will go. Besides, I never gave Mr. Peters a set time when I would be there."

"So, lets eat," Matt said with a hint of urgency, which seemed to be shared by the other children.

"You know where the milk and cereal is Have at it."

Saturday mornings usually meant cornflakes and cartoons at random times, as each child awoke. This warm summer morning was unusual, to say the least.

The television was off and the entire family say around the table to eat together. Terry, especially, enjoyed the moment. She placed her hand on Jake's knee under the table, and he understood the joy she was feeling. He felt the same way and returned the gesture.

After breakfast, each child quickly picked up their dishes, rinsed them, and placed the in the dishwasher without any commotion. They went to their bathroom to brush. It looked like a band of horses at a watering trough, but somehow everyone worked together.

> *"Look at that, Terry."* Jake said with a glow on his face.
> *"Yeah, they have been talking about going to the farm all week. They even mentioned it in their prayers at night."*
> *"It's amazing to see these kids so excited over straw. Video games are taking a back seat today."*
> *"Sometimes, all it takes is the simple things in life to bring happiness, honey."*
> *"Maybe God is trying to tell us to be content with the simple things."*
> *"You work so hard to provide for this family. Sometimes, I think you want more things for us, than we really need."*
> *"I just want you to have the best. You guys mean everything to me."*
> *"Don't you get it? If we have each other, we have everything. Just look at our children today."*
> *"This morning has been amazing just watching them. They sure are focused."*
> *"Are you coming with us"*
> *"I think I will use this time to get caught up on a few things, Jake. You guys have fun."*
> *"Everyone ready?"*
> *"We're ready, dad. Let's go."*

Jake went out to his truck to clear out the clutter on the back seat. He planned on taking the van, but since Terry was not coming, the truck would do fine. Besides, Jake's tools were already loaded. The children piled in, and off they went. Making the trip to the farm was not like going to work. It was almost like taking the family to the theme park, except for the fact that Jake would be paid to have fun. The children beamed with excitement and it warmed Jake's heart.

Upon arrival, Jake noticed the gate was still locked.

"I guess we are the first ones here, kids."

Jake stopped to unlock and swing the gate open. Then he drove to the house, leaving the gate open, expecting BJ to arrive at some point. The kids jumped out of the truck and ran to the barn.

"Open her up, dad. We can still play on the hay." Matt said with a smile, also share by the others.
"Are you sure you will be all right, guys?"

Each child nodded as Jake unlocked the doors. When he pushed them open, he saw the tractor facing out. The wagon was connected and loaded with hay.

"Look at the size of that hay," Matt blurted.

The heap on top of the wagon had been formed with bales of hay. They were stacked two high against a wooden rail that lined the outside of the wagon. Inside the bales were loose hay or straw several feet above the bales. Apparently, Bob had made great preparation for the ensuing hayride that morning. The tractor was ready to go.

"We can climb up the ladder to the loft and jump into the pile on the wagon," Alicia added.
"Let's go." Diana, Nicole and Matt said in unison.
"Hold your horses. I think we should wait for Mr. Peters. He may have other ideas about the straw on the wagon.

Jake had no sooner got the words out of his mouth, when Bob pulled up near the barn. BJ was with him.

"You guys are here bright and early," Bob grinned.

"These kids couldn't wait for the sun to rise."

"I remember being like that when I was their age. The old wagon is loaded and ready to go.

"We were about to climb up to the loft and jump into the pile, Mr. Peters," Matt said, while the others smiled with agreement.

"Well then, kids go ahead. Your dad and I need to go inside the house for a few minutes anyway. By the way, this is BJ. He will be working with your dad today."

After a quick greeting, Matt, Nicole, Diana, and Alicia ran to the ladder. BJ watched them make their first leap before joining his uncle in the kitchen of the farmhouse.

"I think we can save the existing cabinet facings. I bought some pine boards to use as facing on the island cabinets, along with some sanded plywood for the cabinets, themselves. What do you think?"

"I think we can remove the facings and refinish them as well. The paint looks pretty thick, so they will need to be stripped down to bare wood."

"My thoughts as well. I brought my belt sander, orbital sander, router, planing tool, and sandpaper. My table saw is set up outside with an extension cord as well."

Just then, BJ walked in. Bob explained the work that needed to be done and then headed out to the barn.

"I trust you guys can figure it all out. I will take those kids out for a ride. Betsy needs a workout."

"Betsy?"

"Yeah! You said the tractor was a she. I named her Betsy. I don't know why. I just like the sound of it."

"*So, BJ, have you ever done any carpentry work before?*" Jake asked.

"*After my mom died, I lived here. Uncle Bob let me help him. I made a dresser, which is upstairs. He told me to take it with me after my aunt died, but I don't have room for it right now. I am sharing a small apartment with a friend.*"

"*Upstairs, huh? Can I see it?*"

"*I guess so. Come, I will show you.*"

Jake followed BJ to the top of the stairs and into the last bedroom on the right. A wide dresser, standing about chest high, stood by the door. It had two narrow drawers at the top, with three larger ones below.

"*You made this?* Jake said with amazement.

"*That's it. It was my first major woodworking project.*"

"*It's beautiful, BJ. You can be proud of it.*"

"*I am, Mr. Wilson.*"

"*Just call me Jake, and don't be so formal.*"

"*Okay, Jake. Uncle Bob spent a lot of time working with me. I learned a lot from him.*"

"*It shows. The details on this chest are amazing.*"

"*That project took a lot of time. But, I think I could another one much faster now. Uncle Bob spent a lot of time fussing over the details with me.*"

"*Your uncle is a great guy, BJ. He has taken me under his wing to some degree as well.*"

"*Yeah! Well, that's my uncle.*"

As Jake stared at the dresser, his eyes led him to a small wooden box sitting on top.

"*Did you make this as well, BJ?*"

"That was sort of a practice job. Uncle Bob had some scrap lumber, and that is what came out. I used it to hold some pictures and papers."

"It's very smooth and shiny. Did you stain it as well?"

"I did everything. My uncle insisted that in order to learn, I needed to do the work. The first time I began staining,, it was a mess. Then I sanded it down again and started over. I used all of those tools, my uncle left in the kitchen."

"That's great, BJ. Now, let's go and put them to work again. Thanks for showing your work to me. I am impressed."

The two men headed back to the kitchen. Jake was more than impressed with the young man's work. He was moved by the man's character. Bob may have been a mentor, but BJ was eager to learn. Jake could not wait to work with BJ in the kitchen. There was nothing arrogant in BJ's voice. He had a sense of pride, but it surfaced, only when he mentioned his uncle's name.

"Here's what we have to do, BJ. WE need to refinish the cabinet fronts and build some new cabinets for the island. I have the dimensions right here, What would you like to tackle first?"

"I can build the cabinets, Jake. I would like that."

"I show both cabinets as twenty-four inches wide and the same height as those under the sink. WE need to match the look as well. Their depth will be twenty-four inches like the other cabinets. I was thinking of making a cabinet to connect them in the back. That one needs to be twelve inches wide, with several narrow doors. I thought it would be a good place to store can goods, sort of like an under-the-counter pantry. The island top will be granite and extend another twelve inches with stools below."

"Sounds great, Jake. I may need your help to rip some plywood, but otherwise, I am ready to start."

"I'll be pulling down some cabinet fronts to sand. Let me know when you need me."

"I will."

Jake worked alone most of the time in his plumbing business. Yet, working with BJ seemed to add something more enjoyable. Throughout the morning, the two carried on small conversations, while skillfully carrying out their duties. Jake was surprised by the craftsmanship BJ demonstrated. Except for a few moments helping him cut the plywood on the table saw, BJ was on his own. The framework for the island cabinets was cut, routed, and ready for assembly before noon.

As BJ began clamping and gluing these frames, Terry pulled her van up near the house. She opened the side door and lifted a large kettle out. Then she carried it into the house.

"Is that what I think it is, honey?"

"That depends. If you think it's soup, then you are right. I tried a new concoction this morning. I guess you can call it chicken noodle, as those are the main ingredients."

"It smells wonderful, honey. This is BJ."

"Hi BJ."

"Hi Mrs. Wilson."

"Would you like some hot soup?"

"That would be great, Mrs. Wilson."

"Don't be so formal. You can call me Terry. I have some bowls and utensils in the car."

"I'll get them Mrs. Wilson. I mean Terry."

"That would be wonderful. Everything is in a box on the front seat."

As BJ left, Terry nodded at Jake, as if to agree with everything Jake had shared about the young an earlier. Her first impression was a good one, though without any de-ja-vu experience as Jake encountered in his first meeting.

"BJ sure is a well-mannered young man."

" I am impressed, too. Look at how far he has come with the island cabinets. I think we will have them ready to stain before we leave today."

"That is impressive."

As BJ entered with the box of bowls, Jake went to see if Bob had returned with the kids. As he approached the barn, he could hear the tractor off in a distance. It sounded as if it was coming nearer, so he ran towards it.

"Anyone hungry?" At first there was no answer,so he shouted again.

"Did I hear you say something about food?" Bob bellowed.

"How does homemade soup sound?"

"That little wife of yours bring some soup?"

"A big kettle. Plenty for everyone."

"We'll be right there my friend."

The wagon pulled up near the house and a group of hungry children jumped off. The once tall pile of hay had been beaten down about half way.

"It looks like the kids have been having fun."

"That they have. That they have, and so have I. You have some fine children here. You are truly blessed."

"That we are my friend. Come on and have some soup. You can see the progress we have made. BJ is doing great."

"He should. I taught him everything he knows about woodworking."

"Yeah! He told me. He showed me the dresser that he made as well."

"He is real proud of that piece."

A makeshift kitchen table was made using on of the plywood sheets and a couple of sawhorses. Matt, Diana, Nicole, and Alicia introduced themselves to BJ. It may have been the hungry bellies or the hot soup, but everyone was thoroughly enjoying one another's company. The kids made small talk with BJ, and he also opened up to them. Jake and Terry enjoyed the moment as well. No television, no video games, or even a radio playing, yet, everyone was smiling.

"So, tell me about your hayride," Jake said with interest.

"It was great, dad," Matt began. *"I think we went a hundred miles."*

"More like ten," Bob inserted.

"There's a wide creek in the back with a swimming hole." Diana added.

"How do you know it's a swimming hole? Did one of you take a dive?"

"I guess you can blame me for that," Bob clarified. *"I told them that it was where I used to go for a swim. During the rainy season it gets about eight feet deep in the center. It's probably only four feet or so now."*

"We used to swing across on a rope and let go." BJ said with a smile. *"There's fish in it, too."*

"Really?" Matt blurted.

"Maybe we can go fishing sometime, Matt," BJ responded.

The farm had produced an abundance of possibilities for everyone over simple things. Terry could not stop smiling, and it was infectious.

"I wish your aunt was here right now, BJ. She really would have enjoyed listening to all of you." Bob said with a sigh.

"She always enjoyed having people over, especially when they all have a good time."

"Anyone want to play in the loft, " Bob shouted.

Each child started to take their bowls to the sink area, but Terry stopped the. She let them know that she would take care of the dishes this time. The well had not been running for a while, so she planned to clean the dishes at home. Playing in the loft sounded like a good idea, so the kids were more than eager to take off.

"You sure have some well-mannered children there, Mrs. Wilson."
"We do our best to instill values."
"Keep up the good work."

By mid-afternoon, the island cabinets were completed, except for adding the shelving hardware. BJ had even completed the pine facing. All that was left was the doors.

"So, BJ. What did you plan for the doors?"
" I will make them like the ones on the existing cabinets. You'll see."

The old cabinet doors had a center portion with a raised design look. Jake was not sure how to reproduce the design, which led him to ask the question. Something in BJ's voice put closure on the question. There was a confidence about BJ, which seemed to fill the room. Jake had removed all the doors and hardware from the existing cabinets. Most of the framing was sanded and ready for painting, but the doors would take more work.

"Hey, BJ. How should I prepare these doors? They must have five or six coats of paint."
Aunt Bertha used to keep some stripper out on the back porch under the bell jars. You need to start with that, but I suggest you do it outside."
"Good idea, BJ. I'll take a look."

Jake found the stripper, just as BJ said. The gallon container appeared full and unopened. Near the well was some old planking that would serve to support the doors while the stripper was being applied. While Jake was brushing on the stripper fluid, BJ brought out a wire brush and handed it to him.

"You will need this to strip the first few layers. Let the stripping fluid set for a few minutes between applications. Let me show you on this door.

Jake watched as BJ skillfully removed several layers of paint. Then he made another application of the stripping fluid.

"Do this one more time, or until you get to the last layer. Uncle Bob has wire brush attachments for a drill to clean up the final curved edges, so they won't scratch. The last layer can be sanded after it dries."

"Did Uncle Bob teach you all this, BJ?"

"Yeah! Some of it when I worked on my dresser."

Again, Jake was impressed by BJ. Bob had demonstrated many things, which BJ learned well. Yet, the young man learned how to pass those things on to others. He took an active interest in Jake. The experience was heartfelt and unique. Jake had never spent quality time like that with his father. Part of the reason was his father's unwillingness to teach him. Then again, he never really knew his father, who left when Jake was five. His stepfather could take on many tasks, but was too much of a perfectionist to teach anyone else, especially Jake. Still, BJ never knew his father either. Perhaps, God was teaching Jake a lesson as well.

"BJ, do you mind if I ask you something?"

"I don't mind. What is it?"

"Well, I was curious about something. Did your uncle insist on teaching you about woodworking, or did you ask him to teach you?"

"Uncle Bob would perform many acts of service for my aunt. I think my curiosity got to him. I was like his shadow."

"So he called you over and asked you if you would like to learn how to do the work he was on?"

"I guess it was hard not to. I think I mimicked what he did."

"It sounds like you took an active interest in learning his trade."

"I guess you could say that. By the way, why do you ask?"

"I never knew my father. He left when I was five. My mom remarried a year or so later. My stepfather did many things around the home, but never asked for my help. Everything had to be perfect,

and I am sure I wasn't that. Then there was a time when I tried to help paint some stairs."

"That sounds interesting. Tell me about it."

"I was about six. Mom was dating my stepfather at the time. We were living in an upstairs apartment with ten or so steps leading up. Mom always complained about how they looked so shabby. Anyway, I found some partially opened different colored cans of paint in the basement."

"You didn't paint them different colors, did you?"

"Every other step. That I did, and at the time I was pretty proud of my accomplishment."

"I can just picture your stepfather's reaction. You must have been in big trouble."

"You got it. But, I was just a six-year old boy. It was something that I never forgot. Maybe, I am afraid to share what I do with my children, unlike your uncle."

"Not everyone is like Uncle Bob. I think he is in a class by himself."

"I would love to be like your uncle with my kids. How old were you when you first worked with Uncle Bob?"

"I was a teenage for sure. Maybe fourteen. It was a year or two before mom died."

"Tell me about your mom, Bj."

"She was beautiful and at the same time sad. She was married a couple of times, but I never knew my dad. She raised me alone, working as a waitress a lot."

"She sounds like a lonely person."

"She had a few good friends. But none of them male. I think marriage had a negative impact for her. She would not talk about my dad. She seemed to harbor a lot of guilt about something, but kept to herself."

"I am very sorry to hear that, but you turned out very well BJ."

"Do you believe in angels, Jake?"

"I believe God sends messengers to help us in some form, BJ."

"Sometimes, I think He sent one to watch over me. My life could easily have been filled with trauma, but people show up at the right time to help me through."

"Like your aunt and uncle?"

"Yes, like them. But, I also feel that I have a special purpose for my life."

"Have you accepted Jesus Christ into your heart, BJ?"

"When I was twelve. I was baptized in that swimming hole. I insisted on that."

"I think that God, surely, has a special task for you on this earth, BJ. You are quite a mature young man."

"I want to serve Him. I guess I am open to about anything, even woodworking. Speaking of that, don't you think we should get back to work?"

"Thanks for sharing with me, BJ. You may not know it, but you encouraged me today. I think that was your gift."

"I enjoyed our little talk as well. Perhaps, we can do this again sometime."

"I would like that my friend.

AN UNEXPECTED TWIST

The work that Saturday went beyond expectation. Terry took the children back early, after Bob drove the tractor into the barn and closed the doors. BJ completed the cabinets and framed the base of the island to accept the dishwasher. The kitchen had begun to take shape Bob asked Jake if he would take BJ home, and he agreed. The last three hours left Jake and BJ by themselves, and they enjoyed the fellowship.

By the time Jake arrived home, the kids were asleep. They went to bed early, as the hayride and outdoor fun wore them out.

"You should have seen them. They were falling asleep at the dinner table. The fresh air was good for them."

"They sure looked like they were having fun, huh?"

"They could not stop talking about it. I don't think the TV was turned on today. I never heard them laugh so much either."

Jake and Terry beamed with joy as they shared. The experience positively affected them almost as much as it did the kids.

"I had a great day as well, honey. BJ and I worked well together. We talked constantly. He really is a great young man."

"I could sense that you guys were hitting it off."

"If my business grows, I would love to hire BJ as an assistant. I think I could teach him about plumbing, and he has a willingness to learn. I have never seen such a desire before."

"Maybe, You could use him on a few jobs that require an extra hand even now."

"I will give it some thought. Any of that soup left? I sure am hungry."

"There's plenty, but don't fall asleep like our kids when you eat it." Terry said with a warm affectionate hug.

Everyone packed into the van and headed off to church the next morning. The kids were still buzzing about their experience on the farm. Terry and Jake just smiled at each other. Upon arriving, the children headed off to their respective Bible study classes, while Terry and Jake met friends at the coffee area. Terry enjoyed setting up a counter with a wide variety of homemade baked goods that were served as well. Conversations with friends over a cup of coffee often lasted beyond the twenty minutes allowed before the adult classes began. This morning was no exception.

"Hey, Jake," Bill Oliver shouted.

"Hi Bill. How's your wife doing? She was coughing pretty bad last week."

"She's too ornery to let that get to her. She's fine now. Anyway, I wondered about your business. How are you doing?"

"Business is great, Bill. I have work lined up for a couple months along with some side jobs. Why do you ask?"

"Tony Jackson and I were talking earlier this week. He is on the town's zoning board. I guess there have been a lot of complaints lately about shoddy workmanship on new construction projects. He has been involved in several meetings this week."

"So how does that affect me? You know my work. I don't cut corners."

"You do great work, Jake. Did you ever get your plumbing license?"

"Not yet. I have been so busy that I put it off for a while."

"You can't put it off any longer, my friend. The board's action insists on using only licensed contractors in the future to land new contracts. How close are you to getting that accomplished?"

"I really don't know. It has been quite a while since I reviewed the new regulations. I think I have a good handle on things, but the idea of taking a test scares me."

"I just cannot picture anything scaring you."

"Yeah! Well, I am better with my hands then using my mind. The questions don't bother me, only the answers."

The two men smiled.

"How soon will the zoning board make it official?"

"I'm not really sure, but Tony gave me the impression that it would be soon. I gotta go to my class now. WE can talk later."

Jake gulped down his coffee and headed for his class as well. The thought of getting his license sent chills up his spine. He could do the work with the best of them, but passing a test was something else. Jake managed to get through school, but not without help. Bill's unexpected news left a hole in Jake's belly big enough for an elephant tom walk through, or at least it seemed that way. He tried to listen to his Sunday school teacher, but his mind kept drifting. A cold sweat crept down his neck the more he thought about getting his license. It was something that he truly desired to do, but actually accomplishing it was something else, indeed.

After his class was over, he met Terry in the church narthex. She enjoyed a separate class with just women. She could see the anguish on his face and sensed some concern in his voice.

"What's wrong, honey. You look like you've seen a ghost."

"Not a ghost, exactly, but I am frightened."

"What are you scared about?" Terry placed her arm around his neck and could sense the tension.

"Bill Oliver and I had a discussion over coffee. The town board is concerned about a lot of shoddy contractor workmanship, lately."

"They can't mean you."

"No, not me specifically. The housing contractors are using cheap labor to cut costs. New owners are complaining."

"It has also affected your bids, hasn't it?"

"I have had to reduce profit margins to stay competitive, but that's not the problem. The board is going to insist on using only licensed contractors to do the work. That means that I will have to get that piece of paper to stay in business."

"So, what's the problem. You can do that."

"I hate tests, honey. I always have. Even when I knew that right answers in school, I would make silly mistakes. The thought of test-taking petrifies me."

"I believe in you, Jake Wilson. You need to believe in yourself."

"I wish I could find a way to be calm."

"Let's pray about it tonight, honey. I'm sure that God can remove your fears."

"I love you Mrs. Wilson. You are so right. I need to let God work in this area of my life. I'm sure He will provide peace for me."

ANSWERED PRAYER

Monday morning came sooner than expected. Although, Jake asked God to help him with his fears, he still tossed and turned a lot during the night. One part of him stayed focused on the work at hand, while another side agonized over passing an exam. Jake had reviewed the plumber's manual several times. Often, he refer to it when any"how to" question arose on anything unfamiliar in his trade. Still, the words he muttered to himself all day were *"Let go, let God."*

He did not see Bob's truck at the site that morning. The plumbing materials would be delivered later that week and Jake wanted to confirm the time, so he could meet the truck. Shortly before noon, Bob pulled up and hit his horn with two quick beeps. Jake knew the sound and put his tools aside to go meet Bob.

"What's all the racket, bob?" Jake said with a slight grin.

"The sewer's coming through."

"You mean at the farm?"

"Exactimundo my friend. It's coming within three-hundred feet of the house."

"That's great. Are the water and phone lines coming as well"

"Everything the housing tract across the street is getting, we can get. That old well and septic system can be only a memory."

"It'll cost a little to run three-hundred feet, but a lot less than repairing the septic. You can also add a garbage disposal in the plan as well. That's great news."

"How soon will the sewer lines extend to your property?"

"I was told that they are laying about two-hundred feet a day and are less than a quarter mile away now. At that rate, the lines should reach my property within the next two weeks."

"I need to talk to someone doing the work to see where we can tap into the line."

"Already did. I met my friend at the property and painted some sod to mark the spot. Here's the information."

"All we need is a trench dug. I will measure the run to the house and add the conduit to the materials order. If your supply house has everything, then it can be delivered with the rest of the materials."

"I will take care of the trench. The small dozer at the site is available on weekends. I was thinking that you can lay the piping from the house to within ten feet and I can cover that part of the trench. I don't want an open trench for very long."

"Sounds like a plan, a good plan. We can lay the sewer and water line."

Jake marveled how quickly everything was coming together. He had a lot of work to do inside the house, but the biggest delay was now eliminated. With no one living in the house, Jake could gut the old black iron pipes and run new without interruptions. If people were living in the house, the work would take much longer in order to keep some level of comfort in the process. With everything going smoothly, he could complete the installation within a month, even working part time.

The two men broke for lunch and discussed the work at the farmhouse. Material delivery would come that Friday, and Jake agreed to be there when it arrived.

"I haven't seen BJ since Saturday, but he sure enjoyed working with you, Jake."

"Now how do you know that?"

"Trust me, I know. He is my nephew after all."

"Well, when you see him, please let him know that the feeling was mutual. He is a fine young man. I even discussed with my wife, the idea of hiring him to help me on occasion with plumbing work."

"That would be a great idea. BJ loves to learn new things. I showed him how to change a toilet float once, but that was the extent of my plumbing experience with him. I think that job took all day." Bob laughed as he thought about all of the trips that he taken to the local plumbing supply house.

"You never start a plumbing job on Saturday afternoon." Jake added with a snicker.

"Never. I learned that the hard way."

During lunch, Bob sensed that there was something bothering Jake. He waited for him to share what it was, but Jake avoided talking about anything personal. The short moments of humor did little to remove the look of concern on Jake's face. Finally, Bob asked, *"What's the matter?"*

"What do you mean?"

"I can see anguish written all over your face my friend. Fess up. What's bothering you?"

"Taking a test, Bob. Taking a test. That's what is troubling me."

"That's all. I was really worried for a second," Bob said lightheartedly.

"You don't understand. I would rather wrestle a mountain lion."

"So what is the test you are talking about?"

"I need to get my plumber's license, and soon."

"Oh, I guess you already heard about the meetin' then. Don't worry. You got time. That ordinance won't take affect until the next quarter. Besides, you can pass that test with flying colors."

"It's not the knowledge that I am worried about. I have always choked on tests. It is as though my mind wanders into a different zone or something."

"Yeah! I used to be that way, until a high school friend put me at ease."

"How'd they do that?"

"Jake, your fear comes from different areas of your life. Has someone close ever called you stupid, or said that you'll never amount to anything?"

"I suppose. Classmates can be cruel. My stepfather did little to encourage me either."

"See! That's it. You need someone to be your encourager."

"Terry tries to do that."

"Wives don't count, Jake. Men need other men. I think we communicate better when it comes to some things, especially in work related discussions."

"Maybe, but what did your friend do for you?"

"I dreaded those high school SATs, Jake. My friend brought over several old tests for me to review. He would read each question, while I selected one of the four possible answers."

"And that worked?"

"It was more than that. He had the right answers available. After each question he would poll me to see if I was sure. When I was, he responded with a thumbs up sign."

"And when you were wrong ..."

"He asked what I was thinking and how I came up with the selection I had made. He helped clear away the cobwebs for me. My thinking became much clearer after several repetitions with other SAT tests."

"So, do they have any recent plumbing license tests here in Florida?"

"They must. The test changes each year so that people cannot memorize an answer sheet, should it fall into the wrong hands. I'll see if I can find some for you."

"That would be great, but then I have to find someone to help me like your friend."

"Don't worry about a thing. I have just the right person for you. You'll see."

There was something in Bob's tone of voice that reassured Jake. Was God answering his prayers? At least that was the question that came to Jake's consciousness. The lines of worry that Bob saw on his face seemed to go away. Yet, who would be his mentor?

Upon arriving home, Terry greeted her husband at the door. She felt concern for him all day and wanted to ensure that he had a safe place to fall when he arrived. She did not see the worry on his face or feel any unusual tension in his back. Jake seemed to be at peace and even Terry was taken by surprise.

"You must have had a great day, honey."

"I had a wonderful day, sweetie. Thanks for the warm greeting to finish it off."

"So, what happened? You were pretty uptight when you left this morning."

"I think I just let God be God. At least that's all I remember saying to myself all morning. 'Let go let God' were the words. I think I try to use Him when all my efforts fail, first."

"That sounds human to me, honey."

"He's so much bigger than I am. I should just let Him be who he is. Besides, He wants to be there for us."

"Come on, honey, something happened today. Tell me. God did something, or you wouldn't be so perky right now."

"I shared with Bob over lunch about the license testing. You know, at the farm on Saturday, BJ asked me if I believed in angels. Could Bob be my angel?"

"I'm sure God can use anything or anyone to act as His messenger, honey."

"Bob sure has been great. He talked about having a similar problem when he was in school."

"How did he overcome it?"

"He found a friend who would help him, someone to bounce ideas off. The friend was like a teacher going over test questions before the actual test. In Bob's case it was the SATs."

"I remember doing that with Stacy. We would get old tests at the bookstore and question each other. I think it helped both of us."

"I just don't know who will be that person. Bob said it should be of the same gender. Sorry, honey. I know you want to help."

"We'll find someone."

"No! That's just it. Bob has someone already in mind. That's why I asked about angels. I think he is mine."

"I wonder who he has in mind."

"Yeah! I wonder too. Anyway, after Bob left I had an amazing feeling of peace fall over me. It was as though all of my worries were being carried away on a cloud. It's hard to explain."

"No need. It is written on your face. I saw you this morning, remember?"

"That bad, huh?"

"Supper will be ready shortly."

Jake greeted the children as he headed for the shower. They were playing a board game on the living room floor. The scene was surreal to Jake, as he wondered what he had done to deserve such great kids. They actually loved being together. There was no sibling rivalry, at least none that he had observed. He lightly pinched himself to see if it was all a dream. There was great peace in the Wilson house.

As usual, dinnertime was sharing time. The children shared something about their day. Each one included something about a friend that was good.

As they spoke, Jake thought about Bob's words of the day. He wondered who would be the man to help him with his testing.

"You guys have a lot of friends in school, don't you," Jake asked his children.

"Yeah, Dad." They almost said in unison.

"Friends are really great, huh?"

Alicia responded, *"They're the best, Dad. I can always count on Joanna when something is troubling me. Somehow, she makes it all good."*

"Even you guys are great friends. I watched you playing your game together when I came home. You really enjoy each other's company."

"I just like to win," Matt said with a smile.

The sibling rivalry began to surface, but there was still a sense of admiration between them. Jake looked at Terry with a sigh.

"What did we do to deserve such great kids, honey?"

"Maybe, we didn't do anything. We have come through a lot and have a long way to go. But, one thing is certain. We are not alone. God has opened every door. I was married to a wife beater and then married an ex-con. After I gave my life to Christ," she added while love tapping her husband on his knee.

"Things have really turned around for both of us since we've been baptized. I know God has had His hand in it. Still, I wonder who He has planned to be my encourager so I can pass that test."

As Jake pulled into the work site the next morning, Bob ran to meet him. Jake rolled down the window of his truck and returned the greeting.

"Hey, Bob. What's up?"

"You're up, Jake. I talked to your new friend last night. Not only will be help you pass your test, but he wants to help learn your trade. You don't even have to pay him."

"Sounds too good to be true. Are you going to tell me who this person is or keep me in suspense?"

"You'll see soon enough my friend. He will meet you on Friday afternoon, when the delivery truck shows up at the farm. I was told it would be sometime after three PM."

"Do I know this person?"

"Got to go. It's raining out here."

The suspense was killing Jake. Then he muttered, "Let go, let God," over and over to himself. Soon, he was calm and completed the work he had planned for the day. The thought of who would help him on Friday popped into his head several times during the day, but any anxiety was quickly relieved. God was in control, and that was good enough for Jake.

THE DELIVERY

riday afternoon came quickly, and Jake was well ahead of his goals for the week at the site. Leaving early to meet the truck was no problem. Without the focus on his work, the thought of who would meet him at the farm began to resurface. Upon arriving, he unlocked the gate and opened it. Then he drove to the front of the barn, where he planned to clear an area for the materials. As he worked, he heard the sound of a diesel engine and stepped outside to motion for the truck to back up to the barn.

Shortly afterwards, another vehicle pulled into the yard. Jake, initially, could not see the driver and did not recognize the car. It was at least ten years old and could use a good coat of paint. Jake continued to assist the delivery truck driver in storing the materials. Then a man entered the barn. It was BJ. Jake didn't think anything about the visit, since BJ was sort of family.

> *"Hi, Jake."*
> *"Hi BJ. What brings you here?"*
> *"I came to help. Uncle Bob says you can use it."*
> *"Sure! Grab that end of the bundle of pipes."*
> *"You got it. So what's this I hear about you needing a tutor?"*

Just then, Jake nearly dropped his end of the bundle. The man sent to help Jake pass his test was Bob's nephew. Jake wondered for a moment, why Bob would recommend BJ, but those thoughts faded quickly. The two men completed the unloading process and sat down on the pile.

"So, BJ, whose idea was this anyway."

"Sort of mutual, I guess. I really enjoyed working with you on Saturday and shared that at length with my uncle. He suggested that we should talk. I would love to learn plumbing as well."

"Last Saturday was great for me as well. You are an amazing young man. I love your attitude to want to learn, and you really apply yourself. My wife and I even talked about hiring you to help me from time to time."

"I would love that, but you don't need to hire me. I will work for the experience."

"As long as I have the means, I will pay. You know more about carpentry, so maybe we can help each other learn a new trade."

"It's a deal. Now, my uncle gave me copies of three of the last four plumbing license exams. When do you want to start?"

"I don't know. I need to start soon."

"Okay, lets begin right now. First, I want to cover some basic test taking skills that I learned. Multiple choice questions have four possible answers, but you can often eliminate at least one or even two."

"So you are saying that I could get thirty-three to fifty percent by just guessing. That's a big help," Jake replied cynically.

"No, Jake. You know your trade. I am sure of that. But, you will have a handful of questions where the answers sound pretty close and you have to decide which one to choose."

"So you are going to help me make better choices on the tough questions?"

"You got it. First, anytime you see the word 'never' or 'always' in an answer, remove it as a possibility when in doubt. That always worked for me."

"You just used the word 'always' as the right answer. I'm confused."

"You're funny. I should have said that trick usually worked for me. Now, second, the words 'all of the above' is often the wrong answer. Two of the answers may look right, so people may make this selection, because they are unsure of the third choice. Don't fall into that trap, either. Make your best guess between the two answers that seem right."

"I'll try to remember that."

"Third, select the letter 'C' if available and one of your choices when guessing. Statistically, it has the highest percentage of all the answers with 'D' being the lowest. I used the tests that my uncle gave me to verify my findings."

"You're a pretty smart young man. How come you are not studying to be a doctor?"

"I applied myself in school, but I wanted to help my mom as well. I picked up extra money doing odd jobs. I even worked a lot for my uncle. I just like working with my hands. Maybe, someday, I will find my real niche."

"You sound like me in some ways, except for the applying myself in school part. Any job that I enjoyed involved working with my hands. But, you can use your mind. Usually, that pays a whole lot more money."

"Money is not everything. Mom never had much and we survived. I felt loved. I sure miss her, though."

"Your mom sounds like she had a hard life, but she was a good mother."

"The best. She was the best. Now, do you understand what I said about test taking?"

"I think I got it. Let's see now. Avoid 'always/never' answers, 'all of the above' is usually a trap, and pick 'C' when stumped. Is that it?"

"You got it. Now let me get a test from my car."

"That's a car. I thought it was an old shoe box."

"It may look funny, but it runs great and is paid for." BJ returned the wry smile.

For the next ninety minutes, the two men went over last year's test. BJ would ask the question, and before the multiple choice answers were even read, Jake blurted out many answers. BJ would reread the question with the answers and for the most part, Jake was clearly on top of his game. But, a few of the questions had answers that sounded close. BJ would reread each answer and then have Jake eliminate the ones that were clearly wrong. Usually, that left Jake with a fifty-fifty choice. By applying BJ's multiple-choice principles, Jake was able to make the right guess well above the fifty percent average.

"Now lets see what your score would have been. Out of one hundred questions, you got ninety-three correct."

"I think seventy is passing, isn't it"

"You passed with flying colors. All of the questions that you were sure about were correct. You know your stuff. Now lets look at the questions where you had to make a choice. You only had two questions where you could only eliminate one possible answer. You got one of those correct."

"Fifty percent is better than thirty-three, huh?"

"You bet. By the way, the one you answered correctly was the letter 'C.' You had thirty-six questions reduced to two possible answers. Out of those you correctly chose thirty answers."

"Eighteen would have been average, so I was well above average."

"You were in the stratosphere at over eighty percent."

"I used your three suggestions, and it really worked."

"We will try it again on another test, but you would have passed with flying colors today, even if you were average with your guessing.

You would have received an eighty or eighty-one. You are going to pass that exam, Jake. You are."

"I surely hope so. Have you any plans for dinner?"

"If that's an offer to come and eat your wife's cooking, then I'm in. That soup she made last Saturday was terrific."

"I will tell her you said that, and have her set another place at the table tonight. We would all enjoy your company. Oh, and thanks for our first tutor lesson. I feel at ease."

Jake closed up the barn, locked the gate behind them, and headed home. BJ followed close behind. Terry was alerted over Jake's cell phone to set an extra place for dinner, which was not a problem. Spaghetti was on the menu, and there were always plenty of leftovers in their family. Terry was surprised to learn that BJ was Bob's choice to mentor Jake, but eagerly welcomed him to their home for dinner. Guests were rare at the Wilson house, but always appreciated.

When the kids saw the extra place setting at the table they also got excited.

"So mom, is Bob joining us for dinner?"

"No, Diana. Your dad is bringing BJ over."

"That's cool," Matt added. I like him.

Alicia and Nicole were also excited. They had noticed BJ watching them play in the loft on Saturday. They waved at him and he waved back with a warm smile of his face. There was something about that moment that felt good. In short, everyone was pleased. Within minutes, the guest had arrived. After several warm friendly greetings and a trip to the washroom, dinner was served.

Alicia prayed for the food and added a thank you for sending BJ to join them. The dinner table had the usual barrage of sharing what happened in his or her day. BJ enjoyed listening to each account, as Terry could tell by his bright smile. He was right at home. The girls were a bit withdrawn at first, until BJ offered a gentle nudge. There was something about his demeanor or his voice that instilled a sense of peace. Later, Jake and Terry shared about the experience. Plumbing supplies were delivered to the farm along with a special delivery from God. At least that was their conclusion. Even the drain pipes, which Jake added to the material's list, were in stock and delivered.

THE WORK BEGINS

Terry cleaned up the kitchen, though the children did their part before going to the living room to play a game together. BJ followed suit by picking up his dishes and utensils, despite Terry's urging to let her clean up for him. Jake and BJ proceeded to play a game of Yahtzi with the kids on the floor in the living room. It was a game where six could play, and luck ruled over skill. BJ fit right in. He didn't seem to care who won, unlike the rest of the kids. But, Terry could see real joy in his face as he played.

"Lets see. Diana won with three hundred thirty points. Nicole was second with two-ninety. You came in third BJ. I was last," Jake said while trying to cast a downtrodden look on his face.

"I never had so much fun playing this game before," Diana added.

"You would say that, Diana. You won," Alicia responded.

"I've won before, but I think BJ Made tonight even more fun."

"BJ and I have to study for a test. You guys can play one more game, but you have to get to bed soon," Jake said as he arose from the floor with BJ.

"Just one more game, BJ?" Matt shouted.

"Perhaps, I can come over again and play. I need to help your dad right now. Would that be okay with you guys?"

"You can come over anytime. I like you," Nicole replied with a heartfelt sigh.

The rest of the clan concurred as BJ stood. As he started toward the kitchen to work with Jake, he turned to make eye contact with the kids. He smiled as if to say that he had fun as well. Then turned to enter the kitchen.

"Mrs. Wilson, I mean Terry, Jake did great on his first test today. He's going to do just fine."

"I know he will. He just needs some confidence right now."

"I'll do my best to give it to him."

"I think you already have. I have some leftover apple pie in the 'fridge. Can I cut you a slice?"

"That would be wonderful. My mom used to make apple pies. They were so good hot out of the oven, especially with a scoop of vanilla ice cream on top."

"I can nuke the pie, and I think we have a scoop of vanilla left."

"Supper was great as well. My roommate and I usually have something out of a can or leftover pizza for dinner. A good home-cooked meal is pretty special. Thank you."

"You are more than welcome, anytime."

BJ went out to his car to get another sample test. By the time he returned pie alamode was waiting. Jake also enjoyed a slice, along with Terry. Then the questions on the test were read. Terry tried to listen, but was busy preparing the kitchen for the next day. As each question was read, Jake responded as he did in the barn. Once again he was sure about more than half of the questions. He applied BJ's techniques as best he could on the rest and the score was tabulated. This time his score was eighty-eight.

"You did it again Jake. You would have passed with flying colors."

"That system of yours really works."

"It has for me, Jake, and it looks like it will for you as well. Lets see now. This time you had fifty-five sure answers. They were all

correct as well. Four questions were down to three choices and you got three of them right. That's a good ratio. Forty-one questions had two choices and you answered thirty-one correctly. That's still a good rate."

"Perhaps, next time we can go over the ones I missed to compare my answer to the correct one."

"I plan on doing that anyway to see if you missed similar questions. Sometimes, just the wording can trip you up. Perhaps, I can update my technique to a few more catch phrases."

"You should be a teacher. You seem to have a gift for that."

"I do enjoy learning and I like to pass on what I know. You may have something there."

Friday's are, usually, Jake's unwind day. The stress from the week is replaced with a high dose of quality family time. After BJ left, Jake was wound up even more than usual, but this time he was not feeling the pressures of work. Rather, his spirits had been elevated to a new and unexpected level. The time spent with BJ seemed to plant good seeds of encouragement, while the weeds of doubt withered. Terry and Jake talked about it until well after midnight.

"I can do this. I can get my license."

"Of course you can, honey. I have always believed in you."

"Yeah, but I didn't believe in me. That was the problem. I don't know what it is, but somehow, BJ helped me believe in myself today."

"That's wonderful. Now get some sleep."

"I will, but first, I want to ask you a question."

"If it will get you to sleep, ask."

"There is something mysterious about BJ. I cannot put my finger on it, but it is as if I know him from somewhere. In many ways we are alike. He seems to press just the right buttons with me. I think he is one of God's messengers. What do you think?"

"God uses everyday people to meet us wherever we are. You asked Him for help, and you received it. The Bible says, 'Ask and you will

receive.' I think BJ is a real person being used by God. So, to answer your question, BJ could be one of God's messengers."

"I think so, too. Anyway, I am getting excited about the possibility of passing my test. That can open a lot of doors for us down the road."

"Let's give thanks to God. It will also help both of us get a good night's rest.

As soon as the sun came up the next day, Jake arose. Bob was going to meet him at the farm to dig the sewer line trench, using the equipment from the work site. The plumbing work would begin. Yet, Jake's thoughts retreated to carpentry. The time spent working with BJ on the previous Saturday had been especially fulfilling.

As Jake put a pot of coffee on, the kids began to stir. They also looked forward to another trip to the farm.

"What are you guys doing up so early? It's barely seven o'clock."

"We want to go with you, Dad." They said in unison.

"Bob and I will be busy working together. I'm sure that he won't have time to pull the wagon today."

"We can still have fun without him."

"I would worry about you and not get my work done."

"But, Dad ..."

"How 'bout this. You can come with your mother around noon. We should be hungry by then and we can eat together, sort of a family picnic."

"Will BJ be there?"

"I am not sure, but I hope so."

"Okay, we'll come with mom."

There was something about their enthusiasm that sparked Jake's heart. The farm had become much more than a job. Once the work was completed, Jake began to feel some concern about how the children would be affected. The land did not belong to the Wilson's. The extra money earned could provide a good start towards a down payment on a home in the future, but the farm was well out of reach of affordability. The acreage alone was worth hundreds of thousands, if not millions. Any idea of purchasing the property was, certainly, beyond reason. Still, watching the excitement on each child's face was special.

Jake headed out to the farm. When he arrived, the gate was open, and he could hear the sound of an engine running near the house. Bob had the small trench digging machine fired up and ready to go.

"Good to see you."

"You're here early. What's the matter? Can't sleep?"

"Slept like a baby last night. Are you ready to lay some pipe?"

"The materials are in the barn. Show me where the sewer is coming through."

"You passed it coming in. I'll show you."

The two men walked down towards the gate. Bob handed Jake a sketch that was given to him by his friend on the county board. It described the type of connection to be used to link up to the sewer line.

"I hope you understand this mumbo-jumbo. It's Greek to me."

"Standard stuff. No problem."

"My friend said that they would make the connection if we get the line to this area." Bob pointed to a three-foot circle painted on the ground.

"If you get that machine digging, we can have that run before lunch. Terry should be bringing that around noon."

"Say no more. That's incentive enough for me."

Jake went back to his truck to grab a shovel. He located the best place to enter the house with the drain line and began to dig. Bob started a trench a few feet away and continued down towards the painted circle near the gate. By the time Jake cleared the dirt away near the house, the trench was finished.

"What would we do without these machines? Can you imagine the labor hours to dig it?'

"Tools are great. That's for sure. What can I do to help?"

"The four-inch pipes are in the barn. You can help me lay them out along the trench. We can move a bundle at a time. It shouldn't take long. I have a roll of copper to add alongside for the water line as well."

"Sounds like a plan to me."

Within an hour the pipe was laid out along the trench. Bob marveled on Jake's skill as he prepared the fittings near the house. Almost as quickly as the trench was dug, it was ready to be covered up again.

"You don't waste any time. That's why I knew you were the man for the job."

"You helped as well. We made a pretty good team today."

"You think?" Bob agreed.

"I haven't seen BJ. Is he coming?"

"He came out with me, Jake. I think he is out behind the house finishing the cabinet doors. He may even be painting them as we speak."

"He sure works quietly. I didn't hear him."

"He told me about how well you did yesterday on those tests. How soon do you want to take the real test?"

"I haven't had much time to think about that."

"I checked with the city, and they test on Tuesdays and Thursday from nine to three. I think they allow two hours for each tester."

"I plan on another tutoring session with BJ and then I will decide."

"Have BJ over for dinner again tonight my friend, and he's ready for that session. I hope you decide to test next week."

"That's pretty quick, but I guess I can make a decision by then."

"What's really to decide? BJ says you can pass the test today if you wanted to."

"He sure has confidence in me. I will tell Terry to set another plate tonight, when she brings lunch."

"I assume that she will bring the kids as well. I have a few more things to show them around here, if you like."

"They would love that."

The pipes had been laid, shortly, before noon. Bob carefully moved the dirt back over the lines, between the house and the painted circle. The only holes left open were at the house and near the gate for inspectors to view. Jake followed along to ensure that   a bed cf sand securely held the tubing to prevent damage, according to the local codes. Upon completion, the two men went to check on BJ.

"How's it going, BJ," Bob shouted as he approached the rear of the house.

"Quite well, Uncle Bob. I have the doors all sanded and primed."

"I can't wait to see them up," Bob added.

"Hi, BJ."

"Hi, Jake. You ready for one final lesson?"

"Just one?"

"That's all you need. Trust me."

There was something about those words that brought peace to Jake's heart. "Trust me," was like the words "Let go, let God," that Jake had leaned on throughout the week.

"I was thinking that we could have that lesson after dinner, that is if you would like another shot at my wife's cooking tonight."

"Count me in. Uncle Bob can drop me off at my place first. I can come over after a shower. What time is dinner?"

"Usually around six, but I better let Terry confirm that."

"Sounds good to me. Did you get those lines run?"

"That we did."

"I should have come over to watch, but I got carried away with these cabinets."

"You can help me with the connections inside the house, BJ. It's just more of the same stuff."

"I would really like that."

Before getting started on the inside work, Terry drove in with the kids. The smiles on each face warmed the hearts of the men as well.

"What's for lunch, honey?"

"I made potato salad, a fruit bowl, and brownies. I thought we could grill some hotdogs. I brought our Hibachi "

"You had me with homemade potato salad, Mrs. Wilson. That was one of my mom's specialties," BJ said with a warm smile.

"I told you to call me Terry. Anyway, I hope my salad can live up to your expectations."

"I'm sure it is as good as or better than mom's, Terry"

"I'll fire up the grill, honey," Jake added.

"I also made a gallon of lemonade."

"This is like a real picnic," Matt said with a smile.

Jake and BJ placed a sheet of plywood on top of the island cabinets as a tabletop. Terry began to prepare the surface with the elements, while Jake cooked the dogs. Soon lunch was served.

"This is a great meal. I really like eating on this island. I can see the possibilities." Bob said this, as he imagined the top made out of granite with a selection of stools below.

"It's big enough for all of us, isn't it," Terry agreed.

I can't wait until the cabinets are completed. Aunt Bertha would have loved it as well. I am certain of that."

"We can measure for the countertop before we leave," Jake said in response. *"I can even rough in the under the counter work today. Would you like to help, BJ?"*

"I would love to."

The rest of the afternoon passed quickly. The children went on another hayride, but this time Terry joined them. Jake started preparing the kitchen drain and water lines, while BJ put the first coat of paint on the cabinet doors. By mid afternoon, the two men were working together on the plumbing work. Jake resisted the urge to do the work himself and allowed BJ the opportunity to learn. It did not take long before the young man was able to handle each task on his own. With the idea of a new water supply coming to the house, instead of the well, Jake was able to leave the existing piping alone. They could still get water from the well in the meantime, but it would be a simple task to drain the old lines and seal them when the transfer is made. Jake explained all of this to BJ as they worked.

Five o'clock came quickly. Bob had lost all track of time as he pulled the wagon into the barn.

"Sorry, Terry. I didn't mean to keep you out so long. You probably have to get home to make supper. Did Jake tell you to set another place for BJ, yet?"

"No, he didn't, but that's never a problem. He is always welcomed, even unannounced. The kids really like him as well."

"That's wonderful. What time should I tell him to come over? I think he will tutor your husband one more time tonight."

"Seven would be fine. I should be ready by then."

"Seven it is, then. I will take BJ home to get cleaned up and get his car."

The kids brushed the straw from their clothes and piled into the family van, while Bob closed up the barn. Terry went to see the work that had been accomplished in the kitchen and say goodbye to Jake. By the time she arrived, BJ and Jake were putting the tools away. The cabinet doors were spread out on the plywood over the island cabinets.

"Those doors look great. They look new."

"Thank you," BJ responded. "They turned out even better than I thought they would. Still needs another coat and then a clear one, however."

"What color are you going to use for the facing?"

"Bob has it picked out, but it will blend well with the granite counter."

"Speaking of that, help me measure the surface area for your uncle. He can order the granite this week if he likes."

"You guys finish up. Bob will take BJ home shortly and I will have dinner ready at seven."

"Oh, I forgot to tell you, honey. BJ will be joining us again tonight."

"I already know. Bob told me. BJ is always welcome. He's like family."

Terry could see the broad smile light up BJ's face as she made the open invitation. She could not feel the tremendous sense of joy in his heart, however. The concept of family to the young man was limited to an aunt, an uncle, and a mother for much of his life. The idea of brothers or sisters was foreign, and Bob was as close to a father figure to him as anyone. Since BJ's aunt and mother had passed away, Terry had taken on the maternal role in his life.

THE EXAM

The evening meal was over. BJ began to grill Jake with the questions from a third exam. Like the others, Jake had a high number of answers, which he was sure of. Once again, Jake passed with flying colors.

"Piece of cake. Ninety percent is your score. Fifty-eight sure answers, although you missed one of those."

"Which one?"

" I will read the question to you, but this time wait until you hear all of the answers."

Upon hearing all of the answers, Jake recognized which one he answered previously, as well as another answer that should have been considered.

"I answered 'A' didn't I?"

"You did. After hearing the answers again, what would you choose?"

"C."

"Why did you choose 'A' the first time?"

"It had the right elements, but after reading all the answers, answer 'C' is more correct, because the question referred to all applications. I answered correctly if the question wanted new installations only."

"Now, that's what I was talking about earlier. You need to read the key words in the question and all of the possible answers. Still, that was the only one you missed, which you were pretty sure of."

"You were going to go over the questions missed. Are you still planning on doing that?"

"I compared the ones missed from each of the first two tests, Jake. I found several of them that are the same, but reworded. Let's go over those first, okay?"

"Shoot."

After going over each question, BJ looked to locate a similar question in the third test to see Jake's response. Once again, he had missed the same questions.

"See that, Jake."

"See what?"

"If you learn from your mistakes, you can actually ace the test."

The concept of scoring a perfect score on any exam was a new one. Passing was always a major accomplishment for Jake. Working with BJ overcame a major hurdle. BJ was so confident in Jake's ability to pass, that the fear of failure was virtually gone.

"Take the test this week, the sooner the better. You know this stuff cold."

"How's Tuesday sound?"

"I will be waiting for you to call on Tuesday night. You will do great."

Once again, Jake felt encouraged by the possibility. Questions of doubt tried to surface in his mind, but were quickly dispelled. If BJ said he could do it, then he could do it. Jake was determined to not let his new friend and tutor down.

Sunday morning was a new day, however. Jake's mind began to be filled with past performances, casting doubt once again on the idea of taking a test.

Jake sat in the church pew, hung his head and prayed for both wisdom and peace. Then the minister brought the message, which pierced Jake's heart. The sermon focused on the disciples and a raging sea. Jesus was asleep below while the wind and waves wreaked havoc above.

Matthew 8: 23 – 27 (NIV)
23 Then he got into the boat and his disciples followed him.
24 Without warning, a furious storm came up on the lake, so that the waves swept over the boat. But Jesus was sleeping.
25 The disciples went and woke him, saying, "Lord, save us! We're going to drown!"
26 He replied, "You of little faith, why are you so afraid?" Then he got up and rebuked the winds and the waves, and it was completely calm.
27 The men were amazed and asked, "What kind of man is this? Even the winds and the waves obey him!"

After Jesus was awakened, He calmed the sea. Then he said to the disciples *"You of little faith, why are you so afraid?"* The words seemed to etch themselves in Jake's mind. The disciples were so afraid of what the wind and waves would do. They feared for their very lives, despite the fact that Jesus was right there with them. It was one of the most amazing object lessons that Jesus ever taught them. Later, Peter would step out of the boat and walk on the water as an act of faith, even if only short-lived. The pastor's main point was that Jesus is with us today and will never leave us if we put our faith in Him. Jake had done that, nearly eight years earlier. Upon leaving the church, he was not going to let doubt get a foothold. He was determined to not only take the test, but to pass it with flying colors.

Tuesday came and Jake went to the town hall to take the exam. Sunday's sermon was still fresh on his mind. He was nervous, but continually prayed for God's peace to fill him. The test began. He had two hours to complete it, which was longer than the time it took BJ to quiz him on any of the previous exams. As he read each question, he remembered his friend's words of encouragement as well as the technique. His confidence soared as he read many of the same questions that BJ went over the week before. The answers were slightly different, but he remained calm.

In less than an hour he had completed the test. The number of questions that he was pretty sure of was far more than any of the tests he had taken with BJ. He placed small marks by each question that had some degree of uncertainty. He now had an hour to review each marked question more closely to see if the answer he selected was the best one. He applied BJ's concepts on fewer than ten of those. The rest he was confident about, almost overconfident. It was as though someone else was right there with him, helping to sort out the wheat from the chaff. It was hard for Jake to explain, but it was as though the best answer was highlighted, even though they were not.

Jake turned his paper in and asked the clerk as to when he would get the results.

"Have a seat, the lady said. I will have your test run through the machine within a few minutes."

Jake sat down. A few minutes seemed like an eternity. Nevertheless, he was happy to know that he did not have to leave that place wondering. The sound of the seconds ticking away from the wall clock seemed loud, although barely heard by anyone else. Five minutes passed, then ten. Finally, he heard his name called. He was directed to the same clerk who took his test from him.

"Congratulations, Mr. Wilson. You passed. You will receive your certification in the mail within ten days."

"Thank you," Jake responded.

"I didn't do anything, Mr. Wilson. You were the one who took the test, which by the way was a first."

"Surely, others have taken the test before me, or is this one brand new."

"I think you are about the hundredth taker of this exam, but the only one to ever ace it. Well done Mr. Wilson. Very well done."

Jake could hardly believe his ears. He thought to himself, "One hundred questions and not one wrong answer?" He sighed. He had never been perfect on anything in his life. The words, *"You passed,"* were instant music to his ears, but perfection was like a dream. Only God is perfect, Jake thought. Then the words of Sunday's message permeated Jake's thoughts. It was as though Jesus was right there taking the test with him.

Jake returned to the work site pondering all that had happened that week. His plumbing business missed many opportunities for landing large jobs, because he was not a licensed plumber. Those words needed to be added to his business cards, truck advertising, and the fliers in the local papers. The very thought of making the additions brought a smile to his face. The very idea that he passed an exam, which he had not considered even taking a week earlier, blew his mind. He couldn't wait to share his good news with Bob.

As he pulled into the job site, he made the customary two beeps with his horn as he parked beside Bob's truck. A few seconds later, Bob came out to greet Jake.

"What's all the racket, my friend?"

"I just came back from taking the test, and your nephew was right."

"Right about what, Jake?"

"He said I would pass with flying colors. He even said I could ace it."

"Does that mean ...?"

"You got it. You are looking at the newest licensed plumber in the city. I can't believe that I dreaded the exam. I want to thank BJ for that."

"BJ might appreciate your sentiment, Jake, but I am sure he won't take the credit. Anyway, congratulations."

"Thanks. This could open some big doors for my business."

"I will make sure that your name is on the approved contractor list with my friend on the board. I will also see BJ later this evening and give him the news."

"When you see the young man, tell him that I aced the exam."

"Are you serious? You actually got every question right? I don't think anyone has ever done that before."

"Yeah, well that's what the lady said, too. She said I was a first. BJ said I could do it. I still cannot believe that I did. Pinch me, to see if I am dreaming."

The two men chuckled and went back to work. Jake could not wait to come home and share his news with Terry. In the excitement, he forgot to call her. Normally, she would be the first person he would call when something new occurs, good or bad. But, all he could think about was BJ and the great encouragement the young man had shown.

REFLECTING THE JOURNEY

J ake's facial expression said it all, when he arrived home that evening. His face beamed with great joy, almost glowing, as though he had a mountain top experience like Moses. He did not have to utter a word when Terry made her usual walk to greet him.

"You passed the exam?"

"Is it that obvious?"

"Jake Wilson, it is written all over your face. I am so proud of you."

"I am thrilled to have to add the words 'Licensed Plumber' on the truck, honey. I guess I should take great pride in that, but I feel so humble right now."

"What do you mean, honey?"

"Everything I feared about taking that test was gone. I was totally calm and focused. It just didn't seem like it was even me taking the exam."

"Maybe you were not alone."

"There was no one else in the room."

"I mean that Jesus was right there with you. I think He can pass any test."

"I started the exam with the intent on reading each question and applying the skills that BJ shared. Yet, the answers seemed to jump out at me. I was certain on nearly eighty percent of them, which would have given me a passing score alone."

"God could have used BJ to help you overcome doubt, couldn't He?"

"Sure He could, and perhaps, He did just that. Nevertheless, all the time I took the test, I felt at peace."

"You prayed for peace and wisdom. Truly, God answered your prayers today."

"No doubt, but there was something else."

"What was that?"

"After reading the very first question, I had faith that everything would be okay. Even when I sat waiting for the grading, I felt God's presence. My human side was anxious to be sure, but inside I was not nervous. It is hard to explain."

Terry warmly embraced her husband for several seconds. Words did not need to be spoken, as the two shared their joy together. Then, Terry heard the sound of water boiling on the stove and released her grip to prevent a spill. Jake took his shower and returned to the dinner table.

As usual, each member shared something about his or her day. The children began to share about school, friends, and other events, while mom and dad listened intently. Then Terry mentioned to the kids that their dad had something to share. Her voice also reflected that the news was wonderful.

"Okay, Dad, what's the good news?"

"Well! Remember all of the work I have been doing with BJ this week, especially here at our home?"

"You passed the test?" Nicole blurted out.

"I guess that takes away the suspense, guys. Yes, your dad passed the test. I not only passed it, but I didn't miss a question."

"I knew you could do it, dad," Alicia said, emphatically."

"I got a hundred on my spelling test today. It made me feel good," Matt said with a sheepish grin. *"You must have felt proud, too, Dad."*

"It was a good feeling, son."

"You didn't tell me that you aced the exam," Terry said with a wink.

"Great job, Dad," Diana added, and each of the others concurred.

"Does this mean that you can make more money and raise our allowance?" Alicia kidded as the other kids glanced at Jake with a look of wonderment.

"Perhaps, but the money is not in this house yet, so don't get your hopes up."

The conversation around the table that day warmed both Terry and Jake's heart. That evening, after the children were in bed, the couple shared together. Jake had been pondering all of the events of the past week and was filled with awe.

"This week has been amazing. My whole life has been amazing. I know that God is behind it all. I know that without any doubt."

"Eight years ago, I made a decision to accept Jesus into my heart and be my guide. At the time, I thought I might even lose you, remember."

"I remember, honey. I also remember wanting to be with you forever. If it meant accepting Jesus, then I would do that."

"I thought you were going to go into a rage, when I told you to move out, based on my pastor's advice."

"I did, well, sort of. I went to give him a piece of my mind."

"Instead, I think he gave you a piece of his, or should I say, God's."

"I must say, that your pastor had a way about him. I mean, he let me go with a sense of hope in our relationship. I listened to what he had to say and it all began to make sense "

"When we got married, Jake Wilson, I knew it was God's will. I knew I was embarking on a new journey in my life, and that God was leading the way."

"That's what I am trying to share, honey. God has been right there all the time in my life. I have experienced so many things, starting with my dad leaving our family when I was five. The gangs, the drugs, prison, and two other marriages were all part of the journey."

"We have both come a long way."

"Today was amazing, yet, I know there is so much more to come. Judge Carter believed in me. Your pastor believed in me. BJ believed in me. Today marks the first day that I believe in me. I truly know that I have put my faith and trust in a God who won't leave me, or us for that matter. I know that God believes in me. Still, there is one piece of my life that gnaws at me."

"What's that?"

"My son, Brandon. If God has been there all along in my life, why would He allow my son to be born in an adulterous affair with a married woman?"

"I can't answer that, but the Bible lets us know that He does allow things like that. Remember David and Bathsheba?"

"Sure, but wasn't David's son killed as a result of his infidelity? I hope and pray that Brandon is alive and doing well. I pray that God has a purpose for his life, as He seems to have with us."

"Jake, we just have to trust and let go of some things. Didn't you say that Brandon was only a few months old when you last saw him?"

"I know you are right about letting go, honey. I try. I have even prayed about it. Yet, I think about him more now, since I accepted Jesus, than I ever did before. I was still a teenager, when I saw him last. I, certainly, wouldn't recognize him today. Still, I wonder. Its as though God doesn't want me to forget."

"Perhaps, God will reveal something to you in the future. We just have to be patient."

"I know, 'let go and let God'. I keep telling myself that."

There was something in Jake's tone of voice that pierced Terry's heart. She could only imagine the anguish Jake was feeling, concerning his son. She reached over and patted her husband on his shoulder, as if to say she understood, though she did not.

"Then there's the farm, Terry."

"What about it?"

"I don't know. There's just something about it that seems to draw me. It's surreal, even a bit weird. It's as though we are being led there for some special purpose, I mean more than just some added income. I have never seen our kids so excited about anything as a group before."

"If there is a purpose, I trust that it will be revealed in due time."

"I guess your right. It's just that each time I go there, I feel warm inside. Whatever it is, it is not something bad. I am sure of that."

"It hasn't been bad for our kids, either, but I worry that they will get too attached."

"Me, too. I told you that there was something about BJ as well. The first time we met, I had this strange feeling that we had met before. Yet, I don't think we ever did. If we are on a journey, then it is a wild one."

"Indeed it has been, honey, but I am enjoying the ride."

"Yeah!"

THE BLACK PIPES

During the Sunday morning coffee time at the church, Jake received several congratulations from other members about being an official licensed plumber. At first, he was surprised by the attention, until one member shared the source of the news. Apparently, all four of the children could not keep it a secret. They were proud of their dad and let others know it. Jake took delight in knowing that.

That afternoon, Jake received a call at home.

"Hi, Jake. This is BJ. Uncle Bob gave me your cell phone number. I hope you don't mind."

"I don't mind. Call me anytime. I guess your uncle gave you the news, huh?"

"He did, but I had no doubt you would pass. Anyway, congratulations."

"Thanks, BJ. I owe it all to you. You helped me a lot."

"Glad to help, Jake. Anyway, I was calling to find out when you are going to work at the house again."

"I am a little behind with my other work this week. I plan on working a couple evenings at the site to get caught up, but I will be out at the farm on Saturday."

"I hope to finish the cabinets during the week for Uncle Bob. I sure would like to learn more about plumbing. Can I help you on Saturday? I won't charge you a cent."

"I think the town will have the sewer connected later this week. That means we can tear out the old black pipes and replace them with new PVC."

"You said 'We.' Does that mean I can help."

"I would love that. Besides, those pipes are heavy."

"I also heard they are quite messy. Uncle Bob was a black mess one time when he tried to clear a clog in one for Aunt Bertha. He needed a good scrubbing that night as well."

"It will be a mess for sure. Meet me there at eight and we can get dirty together."

"Like a couple of pigs in the mud?" BJ laughed.

Jake worked hard the next week to get back on track at the work site. Each milestone achieved meant a paycheck. The time spent testing and ordering materials for the farmhouse had set him back about a day, which he wanted to make up by Friday. The income had been steady, but Jake was living on a week-by-week basis. Despite the fact that Terry assured him that the bills were all paid, Jake tried to stay on top of the money flow.

Once again, Saturday came quickly. The children had been told that they could not visit the farm. Despite a few sad faces, they seemed to understand. The sewer line had been connected, so the work inside the house could be completed. When Jake arrived, BJ was waiting by the gate.

"You sure are anxious to get dirty, BJ. It's not eight o'clock yet."

"I don't like to be late for appointments. I would have opened the gate, but I forgot the key. I have a set for the farm, but they are on my dresser."

"The one upstairs?"

"No. I have a cheap dresser in the apartment."

"I'm surprised that you haven't swapped them out."

"The one in the apartment belongs to my roommate. There is really no room. Besides, I think it will keep better here at the house."

Jake unlocked the gate, then the barn, and the house. The two men carried materials from the barn to the house to complete the drain replacement. Jake took the time to carefully walk BJ through the process, explaining each step in detail. The main line ran through a crawl space under the living room, which was accessible through a removable piece of girding. The space was tall enough to work somewhat comfortably, but a bit rough on the knees. Jake hung an extension light on a beam to illuminate the area.

"We have two jobs to do under here, and if we work together, we should be able to complete this part in a couple of hours. Connecting the water line and installing new copper will be another day. Be prepared to get dirty."

"I'm prepared. I even brought swimming trunks."

"Swimming trunks," Jake said with a look of wonderment.

"I told you about that swimming hole in the back acreage. It's a warm day, and it will feel good. You should try it."

"I guess I can jump in with my shorts. I do keep extra work clothes in the truck."

"So what do you want me to do? I'm ready to learn some plumbing."

Jake began to discuss the step-by-step process to BJ. Normally, he would dive right in and have the old drain line disconnected in a matter of minutes. But, it was important for Jake to provide clear instructions so that BJ would have a solid understanding. In the back of Jake's mind was the thought of using the young man on future projects in his business. BJ was just as eager to learn as well.

"Here's where it will be messy. Parts of these old black pipes have threaded connections. The main line going upstairs was made with hot lead. We need to break the link going up."

"I understand. How do we do that?"

"We could use a torch, but that takes a while. I brought my electric saw with a six-inch blade. One of us will cut through the four-inch line, while the other supports the weight of the pipe below. Do you have a preference?"

"The sawing sounds like the messiest. I'll take that."

Jake was impressed by the choice. BJ was also skilled in knowing how to use the equipment and made the cut with ease. Sections of the pipe were then separated and hauled outside. As expected, the black pipe was filled with layers of crud.

"I don't know how anything flowed through this pipe. Its heavy with sludge."

"These old pipes are notorious for that. I get many calls to unclog drains on older homes, because of it. The new PVC is smooth on the inside, which allows better flow. I told you it would get messy, didn't I?"

"That you did, and I see why."

The old piping was quickly replaced with new in the crawl space. Jake taught BJ how to cut, cement, and support the new plastic pipe, as well as the proper angle to allow the best drainage. The interaction with BJ was especially rewarding, so the added time for installation seemed worth it. Later, they went into the house to address the work there.

"Over here. This is where the old pipe is hidden in the wall. If we open the wall up, we can remove the line and use the holes to run the new ones. Repairing the wall should not be a problem. It could use a new face anyway."

"This part is hidden behind the kitchen cabinets, anyway. The only patching downstairs is between the cabinets and above the countertop. I think my uncle wants that tiled anyway."

"Good observation. Lets check out the upstairs. This drain needs to connect there as well."

BJ's insights added much to the conversation. The one bathroom at the top of the stairs was the likely place to locate where the drain line passed, but Jake knew that it did not align to the kitchen. Since the several new baths would be added, Jake needed to find a central place to run the new PVC. Part of the line had to connect through the roof as well for a vent. Jake saw that roof extension when he entered the house and knew that it aligned with the kitchen.

"Over here. I think the old line is coming up between these two windows. When we are done, the new line connects to three baths. One will be close to here, and another is where the original bath is located. A third will be over there."

Jake pointed to the large room, which will be converted to a master bedroom-bath combination. BJ nodded as if to say, "I understand." The interaction between them was incredible, At least to Jake. Working with BJ was a pleasure, unlike other times when he tried to bring on a helper. BJ's willingness to learn, along with his solid work ethic, was uplifting to Jake.

"So what's the plan?"

"We only need to get the drain line up to this point for now. There will be some reframing for the new baths anyway, and the roof vent can wait. If we open this wall up, I think we can complete this part in short order."

"Lets do it then. Do you want me to open the wall? That saw we used below can do that quite easily."

"That it will."

Once again the two men worked well together. The drain line was run, with the old black pipe removed in the process. As predicted, they were covered with filth, yet thoroughly enjoying each other's company. A drain extension was also added for the downstairs bath as well. Jake was amazed by the amount of work that had been accomplished and it was only one o'clock.

"Ready for some lunch," Jake inquired.

"I'm ready, but I don't think we present ourselves very well looking like this."

"I was thinking about calling Terry and have her pick up something for us, while we start connecting the water lines. What would you like, my treat?"

"I don't need much, but have her bring the kids with their bathing suits."

"Great idea, BJ. The kids will love that. I'll let Terry decide about the food."

"Great! Last nights leftovers would be wonderful."

"In case you forgot, you finished off the spaghetti."

"Oh yeah. Well, I told you she's a good cook."

Jake made the call and Terry agreed to bring the food. When the children heard about the need for swimming suits, they quickly stopped what they were doing. Mom could not prepare lunch fast enough for them. Besides, they had already eaten. The feelings, Jake had shared with Terry the night before, came back stronger than ever. There was something magical about the farm and the connection with BJ. Jake could not shake the feeling that God had a greater purpose than the plumbing work.

The county added a shutoff for the new water line near the entry gate. The copper line, which Jake ran underground, had been connected with the water turned off. The copper coil near the house needed to be brought in to replace the one coming from the well. Jake described this process as well to BJ.

"Have you ever used a pipe cutting tool before, BJ?"

"Can't say that I have. Show me."

"I'll do better than that, BJ. You will cut the copper tubing, while I watch. Don't worry. I will talk you through it."

"That would be great."

BJ followed instructions to the letter. Jake went to his truck and located a main shutoff valve, along with an outside faucet. BJ made all of the connections and by the time Terry arrived with some food, they were ready to turn on the water.

"Looks great, BJ. Nice job."

"You are a great teacher, and you said that was my gift."

"Yeah, well, you are a terrific student. It has been a real pleasure for me as well. Let's go see what Terry brought for lunch."

"First, lets rinse off. Did you open the main supply line at the gate?"

"Turn off the main valve that you just installed and come with me."

"Done."

Jake grabbed a long T-shaped wrench from his truck, and the two men walked towards the gate. Terry watched them intently, as she stepped out of the van. There was something in their walk that warmed her heart. Her husband seemed light on his feet, and BJ matched him stride for stride. They were sharing and laughing together. The discussion the night before seemed to reinforce the feelings, which Jake tried to explain to her. The children saw BJ and began to run towards him, shouting.

"BJ. Wait for us."

BJ turned around and motioned for them to wait by the house. *"Stay there. We are about to turn on the water. You can let us know if there are any leaks, okay?"*

"OK."

Matt ran over to where the outside faucet had been secured. The others stood about ten feet away, in case there was a leak. Matt may have hoped to see one and take advantage of the spray. Anyway, the water was turned on and after a moment of waiting for notification of a leak, none was made. The men returned to the connection, opened the main valve and watched. Then they turned on the faucet. After a few sounds of sputtering, which Jake said was caused by the trapped air, clear water flowed with a rush. They rinsed their arms, hands, and faces. Then the faucet was turned off. Once again, they watched for a leak. None was found.

"Great job. You connected your first water line and all is well."

"Thanks," BJ said with a real sense of pride. *"Now lets eat."*

"What did you bring, Terry?"

"I was making soup using leftovers when you called. I guess you could call it beef noodle ala Terry."

"Sounds wonderful," BJ said with a smile from ear to ear. *"I just love your cooking, Terry."*

"Thank you. That was so sweet. By the way, I have been meaning to ask you what your initials stand for."

"Brandon James, but no one has ever called me that as long as I can remember."

"You should use it someday. It has a nice ring to it. I like your name, Brandon."

Jake did not hear the beginning of the conversation, but turned towards his wife when she called him "Brandon." He wanted to open up a flurry of additional questions. BJ was about the right age as his son would be now, but the possibility of that being a reality seemed so remote. Still, the name left an unquenchable lump in Jake's throat, one that needed to be addressed later. The children were so excited about going swimming, that they already had their suits on and were anxiously waiting for BJ to finish his soup. As soon as BJ completed praying, their impatience began to show.

"Hurry up and eat, BJ," Matt began.

"People should not eat and go in the water soon after," Terry said to her children. *"Let BJ eat in peace."*

"That's some sort of old wives tale. I used to gulp down a meal and jump in. I never got sick, Terry." BJ insisted.

"Still, my children need to learn some respect."

"Hey, guys. I will be done in just a few minutes. Could one of you get my suit from my car? It's on the back seat."

Alicia said she would and left. BJ's words seemed to satisfy the others as they left BJ alone to finish eating. Even Jake was astonished by the interaction between his children and BJ, who had become some sort of big brother to them. Terry talked about teaching the children to respect others, but BJ's words had an instant affect. Before long, BJ changed his clothes and headed down to the watering hole with the clan. Jake gave his approval. The plumbing lesson for the day was complete.

Jake helped Terry clean up. He rinsed the bowls at the faucet while admiring the work. Then he met Terry at the van.

"Honey, I heard you call BJ, 'Brandon.' Was that a slip?"

"No. I asked him what his initials stood for. He said, 'Brandon James.' You look surprised."

"You know that my son was given that name, although I really don't remember the middle name. When I heard you call him by that name, I must say that it triggered some thoughts."

"Like what?"

"My son would be about the same age as BJ. I don't even remember his birthday, except that it was in June. Father's Day was the following Sunday."

"I suppose it's possible that BJ is your son, but highly unlikely. The name Brandon was pretty popular for a time."

"You are probably right, honey. Thoughts of my son still nag me. I may be overreacting."

"You've come a long way, Jake Wilson. God has a plan for you. If your son is part of that plan, He will let you know. If not, then have faith that all is well with Brandon, wherever he is."

"Good advice, honey. You are, truly, my helpmate."

THE BOX

While the kids were swimming, Jake went upstairs, where the drain line had been run. The name "Brandon" kept ringing in his head. As he reached the landing, he was drawn to the room where BJ's dresser was located. He entered the room and stared for a moment. His mind was still filled with wonder. Could this be his son? The thought seemed so farfetched, yet he couldn't shake it. The small handmade box, which BJ said was his test run before working on the dresser, seemed to attract his attention. Jake wondered if it would be a breach of privacy to look inside. "Should he wait until BJ was there? He remembered when BJ first showed Jake the box. He didn't try to conceal its contents and even said that there were letters, pictures and small artifacts inside. Surely, it held no dark secrets.

After wrestling with various options, Jake opened the box. Inside, were some letters with envelopes, some loose pictures, and a few small trinkets. Jake wondered if anything there would give him either a clue or closure to the possibility that BJ might actually be is son. Still, there was something about the farm and their relationship that tugged on Jake's heart. It seemed wrong to go through BJ's belongings, yet Jake found it difficult to resist. First, he held the cover open and read the information on an envelope, resting on top of a small pile of other mail and pictures. The postmark was only two years old, so Jake doubted that it could unlock a secret eighteen years earlier.

Jake propped the hinged cover against the wall and pulled out the envelope. It felt heavy, like a bunch of photographs. Curious, Jake opened the envelope and removed several pictures. BJ was in each of them as a teenager. Bob, an elderly lady, and the tractor could be seen in several pictures. Jake reasoned that the older lady might have been BJ's aunt. Everyone appeared to be enjoying themselves by the smiles on each face. Jake, carefully, put the photos back in the envelope.

Before placing it back on top of the stack, Jake glanced at the next envelope inside the box. Once again, the postmark was only three years old, so the possibility of a clue seemed remote. Still, Jake picked it up and looked inside. There was a handwritten letter inside. The letter was addressed to BJ and signed "Mom." Jake began to read.

To my beloved son, BJ,

I am so proud of the young man that you have become. I have made many mistakes in my life, but rest assured, you are not one of them. We have never had much, but we have always had each other, and that's more precious than all the gold in the world. I just can't imagine life without you.

You know I have feeling poorly, lately. The cancer has taken a heavy toll. I no longer have the strength to help you when you need it. Aunt Bertha has agreed to let you live with her. Your uncle Bob will also help in any way that he can. I hope you understand. Don't worry, I will stay at the farm as well. I just can't drive or do the things necessary for you.

Love,
Mom

P.S. Thank you so much for helping me through the baptism last Sunday at the creek. The act of being baptized with you was so very special for me.

As Jake read, tears streamed down his face. BJ had shared about being baptized. The swimming hole, where everyone was presently having a great time, was the most likely site. The letter may have been the last form of communication BJ had with his mother before she died, according the timestamp. She was proud of her son. Yet, being baptized together reinforced an even greater commitment. Jake took a moment to gather himself. Then he refolded the letter, inserted it back in the envelope, and placed it back in the box. He put the first envelope with the pictures on top and closed the cover.

Jake headed back downstairs. He, originally, went upstairs to plan the remaining drain line connections. But, the contents of the box became a sidetrack. He felt guilty about opening BJ's personal items and wanted to come clean with BJ. He left the house and headed out the back towards the creek. As he approached, the sounds of laughter filled the air. Everyone was having a great time. Even Terry was there observing.

"*Hi Jake*", BJ yelled, just before swinging over the water to take the plunge.

Jake responded in kind, but too late for BJ to hear.

"*Hi kids. Everyone seems to be having a great time.*"
"*We sure are, Dad,*" Matt blurted, beaming from ear to ear.
"*Jump in, honey,*" Terry said with the same enthusiasm.
"*I will if you will, dear,*" was Jake's reply, knowing full well that his wife would not make the leap.
"*They're beginning to look like prunes, anyway. I think it's about time to dry up and go home.*"
"*Oh mom. Do we have to go so soon,*" Alicia responded with approval from the others.
"*That's up to mom, kids, but I would like to talk to BJ.*"
"*About what?*" BJ asked as he climbed out of the hole.
"*Could you come up to the house? I'll explain there.*"
"*Be right there.*"

Although BJ may have thought it was work related, Terry sensed that Jake was troubled about something. She agreed to let the kids swim a while longer, and stayed there to ensure that Jake would not be interrupted.

"So, Jake, what's on your mind?"

"I may have invaded your privacy, and I want to apologize."

"I am not sure what you are referring to."

"Of course not. First is your name really, 'Brandon?'"

"That's what it says on my birth certificate. Why do you ask?"

"I heard Terry call you by that name and it struck a chord in me. When I was about your age, I was married and had a son. His name was Brandon. The marriage only lasted about a year. I was young and pretty messed up at the time."

"You said that you did something against my privacy?"

"I'm getting to that. I left my first wife about eighteen years ago. My son wasn't even a year old. What is your birthday?"

"June twelve, nineteen hundred seventy three."

"My son was born in June of that same year. When I heard you called 'Brandon,' it sent chills up my spine. I could not help wondering if you were my son. I went upstairs to layout the plumbing work and was drawn to your wooden box on top of your dresser. I guess my curiosity got the best of me."

"You opened my box?"

"Yes, and I feel terrible."

"That's okay. I think I would do the same, if it were me. I never knew my father, but I always hoped to meet him someday. I would be honored, if you were him."

BJ's words were a great comfort. Both men embraced and then went upstairs to retrieve the box.

"So, what questions do you have of me?"

"Well, I read the letter from your mom and looked at some pictures in the top envelope. You must have been about sixteen in the photos,

based on the letter's timestamp. I recognized your uncle, but was the woman your aunt?"

"That was Aunt Bertha. I kept those pictures, because they were taken just before she died."

"The letter from your mother was a real tear jerker. I wept as I read it. I really want to know more about her. You were baptized in the creek together, huh?"

"Mom was a special lady. She was too weak to travel, so I had our pastor come to the farm to perform the baptism. Uncle Bob used the wagon to get her down there. The two of us carried her into the water. I will never forget that moment."

"I don't think I would either."

"Mom passed away in her sleep, two weeks later. She had a short moment of energy before she died and wrote the letter. I read it often."

"That's an amazing story. Her letter mentioned that she was suffering from cancer, yet, perhaps, at her weakest moment she had renewed strength. That was, surely, a God thing."

"I believe that as well. It gives me great comfort. Mom is with Jesus. That much I am sure of."

"No doubt she is and full of strength."

"Would you like to see her picture? I have several photos of her in this box."

"You bet I would."

BJ reached into the box and pulled out a small packet of photographs. He began to pull out five pictures with his mother in them.

"Here she is just after coming out of the water that day. Most of her hair was gone."

Jake nodded, but the woman in the picture looked much older due to her illness. Jake took a moment to review the photo, but he didn't recognize her. Then BJ pulled out a second picture.

"This one is mom when I was two."

After looking at the photo, Jake's jaw dropped. It was unmistakable. The confirmation Jake needed was solidified. BJ was his long lost son. Jake began to weep. The tears streamed down his face. God had gone way beyond anything Jake ever dreamed. The journey has been filled with tremendous blessings, but this one seemed to top them all.

"My wife was named, 'Joy.' Did your mom go by that name?"

With those words, BJ began to well up inside. In that moment, both men shared a common bond. BJ did not have to answer Jake's question. The answer was streaming down his face. Jake put his arms around BJ, and both men could not control their emotions. Joy was, indeed, BJ's mother's name. It was also the emotion they felt together as they embraced. No words were uttered for several minutes. Jake tried to gather himself several times, but his emotions took over. BJ had made an attempt to dry off after leaving the swimming hole, but now was soaked in tears.

Terry had gathered the children together and brought them up to the house. At first she yelled Jake's name with no reply, at least not one she could hear. Jake tried to respond, but was still emotionally drained. Then, Terry yelled his name again.

"Up here, honey."

Jake tried to yell out, but his voice was barely audible. Still, Terry heard a whimper and started up the stairs. As she approached the room, she heard the sound of weeping.

"What's the matter, Jake? Why are you crying?"
"BJ is my son. BJ is my son. I mean Brandon is our son."

Terry could sense the joy in Jake's heart and did not need any further proof. Somehow, she knew. She entered the room and put an arm around both men. She had wondered what this moment might be like and the reunion was far better than anything she would have conjured up in her mind. Jake was gripping Brandon like he was afraid to let him go; for fear that he might lose him again. Brandon was acting in a similar manner.

"God is so good," Terry said as she released her grip. *"I think I need to take the kids home. You two have a lot to talk about, I'm sure."*

"I have waited for this moment my entire life, Mrs. Wilson. I mean Terry. I know that you are not my real mom, but I sure would like to call you that from now on. Is that okay with you?"

Terry nodded with approval and then embraced the young man. Words need not have been spoken. Jake watched from a distance as if to capture the moment in his mind forever. The boy, whom he abandoned nearly eighteen years ago, stood in front of him as a Godly man. Jake always wondered if his son would forgive him, should they ever meet again. The embrace with his wife was like an exclamation point. The moment marked a new beginning for both men. There was a lot of catching up to do.

FATHER AND SON TALK

Terry gathered the children and left. It was mid-afternoon, and a warm summer breeze brushed the two men as they sat down on the porch steps. For a moment they were speechless.

"You must have a lot of questions, BJ."

"Call me Brandon, or better yet, call me 'Son.' I would like that.

The boy he abandoned had suddenly reentered his life. That fact alone was a tremendous blessing, but his desire to be called, 'Son' surpassed all expectations. Shortly after Jake gave his heart to Jesus, thoughts of the son he had abandoned began to surface. The rebellious life he knew had changed forever, but he never forgot the poor decisions that he made. Leaving Brandon was on the top of the list. Brandon's words were not only comforting, but also Jake felt forgiven. The healing seemed almost instantaneous.

"Well, son, you must have a lot of questions for me."

"Mom told me about your affair. I know about her first husband and how lonely she felt when he was away."

"He was in the army. Your mom told me many times that it changed him. He was not the man she married. I think I was a good place to fall for her."

"Where did you meet?"

"At a restaurant. She was working there as a waitress. I was a regular customer, and during slow times she would sit with me and talk. We started meeting at her place after closing. I never liked to go home. I did not get along well with my stepfather."

"Mom talked about you a lot. She really loved you. She said that you left, because you thought it would be better for me. I never understood what that meant."

"I was young. I never really knew my father, let alone how to be one. The only life I knew involved crime, and I did not want to raise a child in that kind of life. I thought you might have a better chance without me around. Your mom could get help from her family, but I had nothing to offer. After I left, I got into even more trouble. I even went to prison."

"That explains it."

"What do you mean, son?"

"I always wondered why you never came back to find me. I thought I was just a mistake or something."

"When your mom told me she was pregnant, I panicked for sure. Her husband had to find out. We discussed different options, but abortion was not one of them. The idea of giving you up for adoption was on the table, however, Joy could not give you up. She was willing to face her husband. The thought of the two of them raising you together did surface, but was short-lived. He was looking for any reason to leave your mom anyway, so infidelity was his way out."

"Mom never talked about him. All she talked about was you. She wondered if you ever found peace. She said that you were pretty uptight most of the time."

"I was pretty rough around the edges, son. I did not back down from anyone. Fighting actually gave me a rush, but raising a child scared the daylights out of me."

"Mom said that she always felt safe with you. We lived with her parents for a while. At least that is what mom told me. I was too young to remember. My first memories involved a small apartment above the restaurant where she was a waitress. There were many times when I would do homework in the back so she didn't have to pay for a babysitter. The free food helped as well."

"You sure turned out a lot better than I did at your age, son."

"My grandparents helped a lot. They would pick me up for church every Sunday, while mom worked. I asked Jesus into my heart at the age of fifteen. When I told mom that I wanted to get baptized, she wanted to talk to the minister. We were here on the farm at the time, and her stomach cancer made her too weak to go to church."

"When did your mom accept Christ?"

"She already accepted Christ privately, but reconfirmed it with the pastor when he came over. The idea of baptism was on her mind, perhaps because of my desire. Anyway, I suggested that the two of us get baptized together. The swimming hole was a perfect place. The water was clear and warm at that time of year."

"I wish I could have been there, son. I was baptized before I married Terry. It was very special."

"Jake, I want you to know that I had mixed emotions about ever meeting you when I was a boy. After mom became sick, my feelings changed. Let's say that she helped me prepare for this day, even if it never happened. Mom carried a load of guilt about her affair, but always talked lovingly about you. She told me that she made the decision to be with you. You did not push my mother into making that choice. I think that she wanted me to let go of any grudges I might have towards you."

Jake's emotions got the better of him. He longed for forgiveness from the son he abandoned, and received far more than that. The shame of abandonment, which held its grip on Jake's heart, was released with each tear that flowed down his face. Brandon was extending his grace in a mighty way. The reunion surpassed all expectations from both men.

"I feel so very blessed my son. God has led me to this point, and I see even better things in the future."

"Today has been an answer to my prayers as well. I have asked many 'why?' questions about my purpose and the circumstances around my birth. I am sure I have more. Yet, today I have received a lot of closure. God truly has a plan for my life, Jake. I believe you are here now to help me achieve even more."

"You have been nurtured by a wonderful mother and family along the way my son. There have been many times in my life when I cast doubts on my decision to leave you, but God never left you. I was not a Christian then, but God knew how things would change. I am so proud of the man you have become."

"Right now, I am not sure of who I am, Jake. I am sort of feeling my way through, so to speak. This reunion may be the one thing that changes all of that and gives me direction. I sure enjoy working with you, especially here on the farm."

"Working with you, Brandon, has been a great pleasure for me as well. If my business grows, I would be honored to change the name to include my son. Still, I would prefer that you let God direct your life as He has done so well already. We need time to get reacquainted."

"That we do, Dad. Terry's cooking may provide opportunities."

The two men embraced again. The joy radiating from their faces told a story as well. The journey had brought them together at precisely this appointed time. At least for the moment, they were traveling down the same path.

The Journey Continues

For the next several weeks, Brandon became a regular guest at the Wilson home. Matt, Diana, Nicole and Alicia enjoyed each opportunity to spend time with their new big brother as well. On Saturdays, Jake would teach Brandon various plumbing techniques at the farmhouse, while the other children found ways to entertain themselves. Brandon was able to teach Matt how to catch fish in the creek. The girls learned quickly as well. They often tried to outdo their little brother by catching more fish or at least the biggest one.

Terry enjoyed the new relationships as well. She would stay at the apartment much of the time that everyone else spent at the farm, and then listen for hours to the fun times each child experienced when they returned. During the week, each child handled all of his or her responsibilities with great care. None of them wanted to stay home the following Saturday, which was the potential punishment for insubordination. There was a sense of real peace in the Wilson family, including Brandon.

Fall had begun, and the house was nearing completion. The plumbing work was complete, except for the kitchen sink. The granite countertop would be installed sometime that following week, so that Jake could complete the work on Saturday. This was a week that Jake had dreaded, despite the fact that he would get paid. The farm had been a great place to gather as a family. Soon it would be just a memory. Bob talked about placing the farm on the market for sale. Completing the work left a bittersweet taste in Jake's mouth.

At the same time, Brandon asked Jake to not reveal to his uncle that he was his son. He wanted to handle that task personally. Jake honored his son's request, though it was difficult at times. Saturday morning came and the finishing touches were about to be completed. Brandon was at the farm bright and early as usual when Jake arrived. This time, the children stayed home.

"So, Brandon, did you tell your uncle about us yet?"

"No, but I plan on breaking the news to him today after we are done working."

"How do you think Bob will take the news?"

"I don't know, but he likes you a lot. You guys will have to talk about that afterwards."

"I guess. By the way, you did a great job with the drywall work in the upstairs bathrooms. The master bath came out even better than I expected. One thing we do have in common, Brandon, is our work ethic. We both take great pride in working with our hands."

"Do you think that is an inherited trait, Dad?"

"Perhaps. Then again it may be passed on through observation. Uncle Bob may have been your teacher before I came along, son."

"My roommate never received the hands-on gene. He's a real klutz when it comes to anything using his hands, even when I try to show him. I think I got my skills from you, Dad."

"I will have to ask God the next time I see Him." Jake winked.

The sink was the last item on the list to install. A tall brushed-stainless faucet complemented the rest of the kitchen décor. A garbage disposal was added, along with a counter-mounted soap dispenser. The plumbing work was complete. All that remained was some tile and flooring work for the house to be ready for show. Jake and Brandon stood about fifteen feet away from the counter to admire the accomplishment.

"We did good. Uncle Bob is going to love it."

"That we did, son. That we did." Jake made it a point to emphasize the 'We' part.

"Uncle Bob should be here soon. I think he said something about celebrating."

"I plan on waiting for him. If you want to go, it's okay."

"I plan on preparing the wall between the cabinets for tile. You can help if you like. I know it's not plumbing. Besides, I may be able to teach my dad something in the process"

Jake smiled. There was something in Brandon's words that was uplifting. Jake had already learned a great deal from just observing his son work. Perhaps, it was the very idea that Brandon desired to teach his father something new. Whatever the intention, Jake felt warm inside and enjoyed spending time with his son. Brandon began to prepare the wall to accept the tile adhesive.

"Uncle Bob will be bringing the tile cutting tools. The tiles are in those boxes in the corner."

He pointed towards the storage room at the back of the house. Jake went over and opened a box. He took out four tile pieces, each four inches square. Then he placed them on the top of the counter's backsplash to see how they would look.

"Is this what you had in mind, Brandon?"

"Not exactly, but I want my uncle's blessing before I start. Anyway, I thought the tile would look better if they were placed on an angle. That will mean more cutting and, perhaps, a few more tile, but I think it would set the kitchen off better."

"Show me what you mean."

"Like this." Brandon arranged the tile. *"Do you have a tape measure, Jake?"*

"In my toolbox. I'll get it."

"Now measure between the backsplash and the upper cabinets. What is the distance?"

"Twelve and one half inches. What does that mean, Brandon?"

"First, measure again further down, Jake."

"It's about a quarter-inch more here. I will measure again at the end. Back to twelve and a half again, son."

"We can work with that, Jake. That extra quarter of an inch will show if we are not mindful."

Jake watched his son write down the information. Then Brandon took a few more tiles from the box and laid them out on the countertop at a forty-five degree angle. Carefully, he made a measurement and wrote it down.

"Perfect," Brandon yelled.

"What do you mean, perfect?"

"I don't think we need to do as much cutting as I thought by running the tile on an angle. If we run them perpendicular, we actually will have to cut more tiles."

"I don't follow, son." Jake said with a look of confusion.

"Each tile is four inches square. That extra quarter to half an inch more will look odd if we try to cut that much off the top tiles. It would look better, if we cut two tiles just beyond the middle and use them for the top and bottom rows. By going diagonal, we only need to trim the top tiles and half of the bottom ones. You'll see what I mean later."

"I trust you son. You seem to know what you are doing."

"I learned how from my uncle. The same consideration is used on the floor. If you draw a line down the center and work from there, the outside tiles will be cut the same size to complete the symmetry. If you start from a corner, then the other corner will look pieced and uneven."

"I can picture that. I guess that's one of the tricks of the trade, huh?"

"You got it. Now extend your measuring tape to measure the overall length."

After Jake yelled out the measurement, Brandon had him place the end of the tape at the halfway point. He then made a pencil mark on the wall and recorder the information on his paper. Both ends of the counter wrapped around. Brandon wanted to ensure that the corners would appear symmetrical as well.

"I'm impressed, Brandon. You seem to want to know the big picture before you start. I am learning a lot here."

"Laying tile requires knowing how everything will fit. You may be able to get away with just diving in the plumbing business, but not here. I have seen some messed up work before. Most of plumbing is hidden, but not tile. Uncle Bob spent a lot of time showing me this. I always plan my work carefully. Now hold this chalk line for me."

"Sure thing, son. I guess you want to mark a parallel line on the wall for reference."

"You got it. Hold tight while I give the line a snap. That's perfect."

The time spent with Brandon that morning was etched in Jake's mind and heart. Brandon had the maturity of a much older man. He demonstrated a professionalism that rivaled many others that Jake had encountered along the way. A true sense of pride welled up inside. The two men shared their thoughts and feelings together for another hour before Bob arrived. They learned more about each other in that hour, than they could have imagined otherwise. Both were duly impressed. The idea of having Brandon as a partner in his business began to take on even more validity. Then Bob arrived.

"Hi guys. I see you have the kitchen completed, at least for the plumbing work. It looks really nice. It also looks like BJ is passing on some of my tiling secrets to you." Bob could not hold back a proud smile.

"He said that you taught him everything."

"I taught him a lot, but he can teach me a few things now."

"Did you bring the wet saw, Uncle Bob?"

"It's in the truck, BJ, along with the tile cutter tool."

As Brandon went to fetch the equipment, Jake placed his hand on Bob's shoulder and said,

"He's a special young man. I mean very special."

"That's for sure. By the way, I have been meaning to tell you something."

"What's that?"

"First, how much more work have you got left at the job site?"

"I am looking for another big job. The site will be done in two weeks."

"That's what I thought. My friend on the board alerted me about a new renovation that came through. I made sure you have an opportunity to bid."

"That's great news. Do they have a starting date, yet?"

"All I know is that it is soon. The work needs to be completed by year-end. It's already October. Anyway, getting that license got you in the door, my friend. Great job."

Brandon entered the kitchen with the tile-cutting tool. He had already set up the saw outside near the water faucet.

"Uncle Bob. We made all of the tile measurements and I think we can run them diagonally without much waste. Is that okay with you?"

"What was the height measurement, BJ?"

"Twelve and one-half inches with another quarter-inch of cabinet settling."

"That half inch is a killer if we run vertically. So, lets run as you suggest."

"Great! I will cut the bottom end pieces. You guys can jaw a while until I am done."

Jake wanted to share the news about BJ being his son. He tried to think of something else to fill the time, as Brandon made it clear that he wanted to break the news to his uncle, first.

"So, Bob, when do you think you'll have the place on the market?"

"Pretty soon. I have some people already interested. I don't think it will take too long to sell, even with the down economy."

"My family and I have really enjoyed spending time here. It started out as work, but more of a labor of love. Whoever gets the house should love it as much as we do."

"You really like the place, don't you Jake?"

"I could not have dreamed about any place better for my family. I will miss this place for sure."

The conversation continued for several minutes. Then BJ came in with a small box of cut tile. He directed work details, starting with the application of glue, which Bob handled with ease. Brandon began placing the tile on the glued area, starting at the center of the wall. Jake placed the full size tile as Brandon laid the cut pieces. You would have thought that the three men were completing a race, as everything seemed to go so smoothly. As BJ made the final cuts for the top tiles, Bob quickly placed them. Special end tiles were added complete the work, and the men took a moment to review.

"Great job. It looks symmetrical."

"You took the words right out of my mouth, Uncle Bob. I learned that from you."

"He also showed me," Jake added.

While Jake had placed the full size tiles in place, Bob added small plastic spacers, to ensure that the grout would be even.

"We need to let it set for twenty-four hours. Later this week, I will remove the spacers and add the grout. I will need another day to add the clear sealant. It sure looks great, and I really like the angled look, BJ."

"I learned a lot as well, Bob. It has been a pleasure   working with BJ today. By the way, I will only bill for the plumbing work."

"Speaking of that, Jake, can we settle up next week?"

"Works for me. You two finish up here. I am going to head home. Take care."

"What's that pretty little wife of yours have planned for dinner? We might follow you." Bob said with a wry smile. BJ grinned as well.

"Road kill. She can make anything taste good," Jake said to return the jest.

The work at the house was now complete. Jake drove away with sadness in his heart. The work went very well. Everything was anticipated with no surprises. Even the county water and sewer lines were completed. Still, Jake had an ache inside that he could not shake. He wondered if it was because the farm represented a new beginning with his son.

PAYDAY

As Jake drove home, thoughts of the children playing in the loft entered his head. He wondered how they would cope with not being able to visit the farm any more. What could he tell them? He poured his heart into every aspect of the work as if it was his own home. Leaving seemed so final. When he arrived at his apartment, Terry met him. Somehow, she had similar feelings. The two embraced.

> *"Everything will be just fine, honey. You'll see."*
>
> *"I know. God would not take us this far, and then leave us hanging. He has a lot more for us. Still, I am going to miss that place."*
>
> *"Dinner will be ready soon. By the time you get cleaned up, it will be served."*
>
> *"Smells good, whatever it is."*

Jake took his shower and spent a few minutes with the children prior to being called for dinner. They were playing a game together on the floor. The scene looked very calm. Perhaps, they knew that they had visited the farm for the last time. Maybe, Terry had a long talk with them. Jake sat down and watched them play without bringing the subject up.

Then Nicole yelled, *"Sorry."*

Instinctively, Jake responded, *"What are you sorry about?"*

The others laughed. *"I just sent one of Alicia's men in the game back home, Dad. When you do that, you say 'Sorry.'"*

Jake laughed along with them. The moment became a great tension release. If the kids did not bring up the subject of the farm, neither would Jake. Than Terry gave the call for dinner, and everyone left the game as it was.

"Did you finish the work at the farm, Dad?"

"I am all done, Nicole. It has been a long time spent on one job."

"We're all going to miss that place," Alicia said with sadness in her eyes.

"I know. You guys had a lot of fun there. Mom and I are still thankful for those moments."

"We will still get to see our new brother, Brandon, won't we, Dad?"

"That's a promise, Matt. He's family. You'll see a lot of him."

The family talks around the table tended to focus on that promise. Somehow, the reunion with Brandon had an even greater impact then the hayrides or swimming at the creek. Brandon had made a very positive first impression with everyone, especially the children. Jake's concerns about the farm seemed to fade away.

After the children were asleep, Terry called her husband into the kitchen.

"Honey, remember several months ago when I talked about the passage in Proverbs about the ants and lizards?"

"I remember. A salamander winked at you from the window sill, as I recall," Jake responded with a smirk.

"I thought the message was for us. Those ants never strayed from their goal. They collected food all summer so they would not starve in the winter when food was scarce."

"Okay, how does that affect us, honey? We have plenty to eat."

"That we do, but there are other things that we have as goals."

"You mean like getting a bigger place?"

"That's exactly what I mean. The ants are not wasteful, but we have been."

"What do you mean? I don't buy expensive things, like a new truck."

"No, but you have wanted to. Have you enjoyed the homemade soups that I prepared while you worked on the farm?"

"Sure I have, but why are you changing the subject?"

"I'm not. That is precisely the subject. Fridays had been dinner out, but I made soup instead. You even had it for several lunches during the week."

"You're right about Fridays. I thought you needed a break, or maybe that I needed one."

"I wanted to heed the words of the proverb. Look at this." Terry pointed to the notebook, opened on the table. *This column represents the savings in our food budget since I started conserving."*

"That's a lot of money, honey."

"That's not all. This second column represents the average cost of eating out or pizza deliveries. Since we have not eaten out, its money that we still have."

"So what are you telling me, Terry?"

"Between the savings on the budget and the money not spent on extras, we have started a down payment account. Your regular income has been more than enough to meet our needs. The work on the farm is extra as well."

Jake stared intently at the ledger. The work on the farm took about five months. In that time, Terry cut nearly two thousand dollars from her normal allowance for food. The Friday night dinners out and occasional pizzas would have matched that savings. The work on the farm would raise the down payment fund to well over five figures. Suddenly, Jake understood the lesson.

"You are wonderful. I would never have thought that we could have our own place, at least not in the near future. I can live on soups. I am so thankful for ants." Jake smiled and gave Terry a warm embrace.

"Like the ants, we still need to stay focused. If there is a place out there for us, I am sure God will direct our path."

"That He will, honey. That He will."

Sunday morning had its usual activities. The children went for their various classes at the church, while Jake and Terry gathered for coffee. While, Terry helped others behind the counter, Jake took his coffee to where Alex McDaniels was sitting alone. Alex worked in real estate, which was in an economic downturn. Still, Jake had the idea of home ownership heavy on his heart and knew that Alex was in that business.

"Hi, Alex."

"Hi, Jake. How's business?"

"I am doing fine, but I wanted to ask you the same question."

"There are a lot of great deals out there, but money is pretty tight. This economy has a ways to go. Why do you ask, Jake?"

"Terry and I are saving up a down payment for a home of our own. The kids are getting bigger, and that apartment is not, if you know what I mean?"

"Teenagers need their space, huh?"

"That they do. So what's out there for us and how much do I need to save up?"

"There are a lot of four and five bedroom homes on the market. Many of them have been reduced drastically in price. The problem has been financing. Twenty percent down plus closing costs can get financing with good credit. Do you know your credit scores, Jake?"

"No, but I pay all my bills on time."

"I can check on that for you, if you like. I can also print out a list of houses in the area that might meet your needs."

"I would like that. We will have about twelve thousand dollars saved by the end of this week. How much more do we need?

"Most of the homes that meet your needs start above two hundred thousand. I'd say that you would need about twice that amount to ensure a mortgage, Jake. I can check on some other grants for first time home owners, which might reduce your down payment amount."

"We have only started talking about the idea, so I have time. I would appreciate anything you can do to help. Terry and I just need to stay focused together on the possibilities."

"You have come a long way, Jake Wilson, since I first met you. I think it was eight years ago when you joined the church."

"That it was, and you are so right. God has done amazing things in my life. This past week, I was re-introduced to my son, whom I abandoned eighteen years ago."

"That is amazing. You will have to tell me more about the reunion, but we need to get to our classes. It's been great talking with you, Jake."

"Yes, it has. Thank you for listening, Alex."

"My pleasure, and I will get back to you on the housing questions."

Jake's mind was full of questions as he headed for his class. Home ownership was a dream, but he was exploring the possibilities. Terry was behind him one hundred percent. This would be a road they would travel together and a source of much prayer.

THE COMMONS

Monday morning had a cool nip in the autumn air, especially for Florida. A cold front came through the night before with temperatures dropping into the thirties. Orange groves paid special attention to the forecasts, in an effort to protect their crops. Jake added a sweatshirt to his apparel as he left for the job site. He had about two weeks work remaining to complete the project. As he felt the cool breeze across his face, he hoped that it was not a sign of things to come. Saving money for a house meant maintaining an income. In short, he needed to find more work. That was his prayer. He also contacted a few men from his Thursday night prayer and Bible study group to lift up his vocational needs.

Since he added the words "licensed plumber" to his truck, Jake had seen an increase in calls, which he followed up with estimates. Large jobs seemed to take time, however. Bids are received, reviewed, and slowly sifted. Often, a contractor is called to make a new bid, when the selection process narrows down to a few options. On those occasions, the contractor knows he or she is in the running and needs to make the most competitive bid possible. So far, Jake had not received a request like that.

Then the phone rang.

"Jake Wilson, this is Jerry Harbins from the state's housing commission. Do you remember bidding on the plumbing work at the downtown Orange Commons location?"

"I remember. How can I help you?"

"That project has been given the go ahead. The state has received federal funds to complete the project. I have your quote in front of me."

"Just a second, Jerry. I will pull it out from my files as well. Okay, I found it."

"You quoted twenty-five units. We will be adding another ten. Do you see your bid about the same per unit?"

"I don't see any change in labor costs. Copper has gone up a bit, but I do not see it changing the overall costs by more than a percent or so. Would you like for me to quote the work again, based on the additional units?"

"Go ahead and do that, Jake, but we want you to do the work. You come with great credentials."

"You will have it by the end of the week, and thank you."

Suddenly, Jake had new hope. The complex would take two to three days per unit to complete. Based on a workweek of five days, that would last a minimum of five months. There also seemed to be some urgency in Jerry's voice. It was as if God had worked everything out so that completing the present site would flow into the new one with great ease.

Before the day came to a close, Jake had received several follow up calls. The work options began to fill his plate to overflowing. By the time Jake arrived home, he was enamored by thoughts of being overloaded. Terry could see tension on his face as he entered the kitchen.

"So, honey, how's your day?"

"Unbelievable. It started with a call from the city about the Orange Commons project that I quoted months ago. Then the phone would not stop ringing."

"Did you get the project?"

"I did and it almost doubled in size."

"That's wonderful, but you look so stressed."

"I am, honey. The other calls wanted more information as well. I am being considered for a lot of work. It came so suddenly. I don't think I can handle all of it. I may have to work double shifts."

"Do you think God is leading you, Jake Wilson?" Terry would use his full name when she wanted to make a point.

"Of course I do."

"Then He won't give you more than you can handle. You have to believe that."

"I believe that, honey. My thoughts are on asking Brandon to come on board and help me. I think that's part of God's plan."

"You may be right. Besides, Brandon would make an excellent helper."

"Yeah, and trustworthy. He was not a part of my life for all of those years. Wouldn't it be wonderful if God intended for that young man to fill our lives from now on?"

"God does work in mysterious ways. That we know for sure."

"I was not much of a father to him when I left. But, I did not know my heavenly father, either. Mentoring Brandon in my business would be like being a father all over again. At least it might seem that way. Anyway, I plan on calling him tomorrow to see if that idea is really possible."

"Sounds like a good plan."

"So what kind of soup are we having tonight, honey?"

"I made a roast with carrots, potatoes, corn, and biscuits. How does that sound?"

"Sounds great. Does that throw a wrench in your food budget?"

"Not at all. I intend to make beef vegetable soup tomorrow with the leftovers."

Jake's mouth watered with the thought. Terry had learned the art of stretching the food dollar. There was something about the sound of homemade soup that seemed so much better than any meal at a restaurant. Perhaps, it was the added love. Jake may have suggested dining out once a week before, to get Terry away from the stove. Yet, she appeared to enjoy working in the kitchen. The urge to go out to dinner was gone, at least for the moment. The knowledge that homemade soup was on the menu for the following evening was a good lead in for inviting Brandon over to discuss his business opportunity.

After dinner, and the table was cleared, Jake went back to relax in the living room. The kids continued playing their game and then asked their father to join them to play a new game that could handle five players. Jake was awestruck by the wonderful spirit of fellowship that his children enjoyed. He felt uplifted to be a part of it. Terry enjoyed the moment as well.

After the children were asleep, Jake made the call to Brandon.

"Hello, Brandon."
"Hi, Dad. What's up?"

Jake paused for a moment. They had barely been reacquainted, and his son already called him *"Dad."* The word left an uneasy feeling, and at the same time gave Jake a renewed sense of pride. Silently, he thanked God for the experience and asked for the wisdom to deal with everything, especially with Brandon.

"Terry's planning on homemade soup tomorrow night. We'd love for you to join us."
"You had me at homemade soup, Dad. I'll be there. What time?"
"How doe six o'clock sound?"
"Sounds delicious. See you there."
"Great. I have a lot of things to talk about with you as well. I hope you can stay a while afterwards."
"I would love to spend time with you and mom."
"By the way, Brandon, did you talk to your uncle about us, yet?"

"Not yet, but I will this week. I will see him at the farm on Saturday to complete some interior work. We will discuss everything in detail by then. Don't worry, and thanks for letting me tell him."

"I'm not worried, son. I just don't want to let the cat out of the bag so to speak with Bob. See you tomorrow night."

"Looking forward to it."

After hanging up the phone, Jake leaned back in his chair and reflected upon the wild ride his life had experienced. His father abandoned him and Jake did the same thing to his son. Drugs, alcohol, prison, and failed marriages were like the low points. The journey led him to Terry and a new relationship to his heavenly father, which surpassed everything else in his life. Now the relationship with the son that he abandoned had come full circle and was mended. He could only imagine what lied ahead. The journey had come far from the lowest lows to new highs.

A short time later, Terry passed by her husband asleep in his lounge chair. He had a warm glow about him. Although his eyes were closed, the smile on his face said it all. She thought about waking him to come to bed, but did not want to spoil the moment. She picked up her Bible and began to read for a while. The room was filled with peace. She began reading again in Proverbs, but this time from the beginning. She was reading in chapter three when Jake began to stir.

"Hi, honey. I must have dozed off. It has been a full day."

"You looked so peaceful. I thought of waking you, but did not want to spoil the moment. I was planning on going to bed shortly."

"What are you reading?"

"Proverbs. I'm in chapter three. It sure is appropriate for us today."

"Read it to me, honey, the appropriate part I mean."

"Okay, starting with verse one. The first six verses seem to sum it up pretty well."

1 My son, do not forget my teaching, but keep my commands in your heart,

2 for they will prolong your life many years and bring you prosperity.

3 Let love and faithfulness never leave you; bind them around your neck, write them on the tablet of your heart.

4 Then you will win favor and a good name in the sight of God and man.

5 Trust in the Lord with all your heart and lean not on your own understanding;

6 in all ways acknowledge him, and he will make your paths straight.

"It was as if God was speaking directly to me. He called me 'Son.' I hope you know just how much I love you. I will never be unfaithful. Next to God, you are the best thing that ever came into my life."

"And you in mine. Your business is getting a 'Good Name,' and we seem to be on a straight path."

"Each day, I renew my trust in the one who made it. Even though the new work seemed to overwhelm me today, I still had a sense of peace."

"God is with us on every step of this journey. As long as we honor and trust him, everything will work out. He will continue to direct our paths."

"I have no doubt that he will, honey. No doubt."

The next evening, Brandon arrived promptly at six. He handed Terry a bouquet of freshly cut flowers and gave her a hug. Upon seeing Brandon, Jake thought about his uncle. Jake did not run across Bob at the site. He thought it was odd that he had not seen him the day before either.

"Hey, Brandon. Have you seen your uncle this week? He hasn't been at the work site."

"I haven't seen him since Saturday. I will see him in a couple days, but you will probably see him before I do. I know he wants to settle up with you on the work."

"You're probably right. I hope you brought your appetite."

"That goes without saying. I hope there's enough left for take out later."

Jake and Brandon smiled at each other, almost as if they intended to battle over who gets the leftovers. It was all in fun. Terry assured them that there should be plenty for both of them. During the meal the children shared about their day and insisted that Brandon do the same. After a while the questions each child had for their new brother seemed to be unending. Jake and Terry tried to end the bombardment.

"You kids will have a lot of time to get to know your brother better. Now let him have a chance to catch his breath."

"Its okay. I think I would have a lot of questions to ask as well."

"You might at that, Brandon," Terry inserted, *"but the day will run out of time before you can answer them all."*

"You kids, help your mother pick up the kitchen. Dad needs to have some time with Brandon alone."

The two men went into the living room and sat down. Jake began to share about all of the new work opportunities and how he could use a good helper.

"So what do you think, Brandon?"

"I would love to come and work with you. It beats my present job, and I know I will learn a lot more. When can I start?"

"I will begin a new project the week after next. I could use you then, but you can start anytime."

"The week after next will be great. I can give my notice tomorrow."

"You haven't even asked me about your salary. Have you thought about a figure? I need to look into other things that apply to hiring as well."

"I know that you will be fair in whatever you want to pay me. I consider the opportunity as an apprenticeship, which pays a lot less than a plumber's helper."

"When I first started working as a helper, I made eight dollars an hour. Then I was paid by the job. As long as I completed the work on time, I earned a much higher wage. If I took longer, then my wage went down. Therefore, it was an incentive for me to work quickly and effectively. It also helped me to learn the trade."

"That sounds like a great plan. So eight dollars an hour to start, huh?"

"That was a while ago, Brandon. How about Twelve and we can go from there?"

"Done. I can't wait to start."

"Nor can I, son. Nor can I."

BERTHA'S JOY

The rain was falling heavily the next morning as Jake pulled into the work site. Bob's truck was there, and the exhaust seemed to form a light ground covered cloud as it mixed with the raindrops. Bob was in the truck reviewing some papers with the cab light on. Jake beeped the horn twice and pulled up along side. Bob waved and motioned for Jake to jump inside his cab. Jake obliged.

"Good morning, Jake."

"Good morning to you, Bob, despite the downpour."

"We can always use some rain. I'm sure that the orange growers will agree, anyway."

"I haven't seen you around lately."

"I had some business to take care of downtown, Jake. I didn't forget you. By the way, I cannot believe the difference a little plumbing makes to the farmhouse. There is one thing left that I think you forgot to complete."

"What was that?"

"The well. You removed all of the old piping in the house, but what should we do with the well? It still pumps water."

"You're right. I thought with the new public water line, you might want to just cover the well. Did you have something else I mind?"

"A new owner might want to use the well water for crops or livestock. I was thinking that we could connect a line to the barn for now and keep the old pump, if it's still in good working order."

"I can do that for you. By the way, I am hiring BJ to help in my plumbing business. That could be a good apprentice job for him."

"I am so pleased that you hired him, Jake. Can we get the work done on Saturday?"

"Saturday works for me."

"Great. Pick up the materials. I left that order open for you. Also, submit a final labor charge to me and include Saturday's work. Don't forget to include hours for BJ."

"I will check on the materials today."

"Great! See you on Saturday. Oh, and bring those kids. The wagon is still loaded and waiting. I'll have the trench digging machine ready as well."

The idea of bringing the kids one more time to the farm left Jake feeling a bit uneasy. They seem to have adjusted to the fact that the farm was just a good place to visit. Still, Jake would pass the request on to his family for consideration, starting with Terry.

"Hi Honey. I saw Bob today."

"Did he pay you for the work?"

"Not exactly. I have one more piece to complete on Saturday. I didn't think about the well after the town's water came through. Anyway, he wants me to make it functional for the barn."

"So, you'll be done on Saturday?"

"Yes. Bob wants to give the kids another hayride. I told him that I would pass it by you. I'm sure they would enjoy it, but you decide."

"I will talk to them first. Then we can decide together."

Jake passed the living room and noticed that all four children were once again playing a game together. He stood and watched for a moment, admiring the view. He thought about the dysfunctional relationships in his childhood and was amazed by the difference. Alicia and Nicole had been received better than he could have ever dreamed. God had led him from a life of violence to one of real peace, and Jake acknowledged Him in that moment.

At the dinner table, Terry brought up the hayride invitation. Without hesitation, each child gave a big acceptance of the idea. Jake informed them that it might be their last time on the farm, and everyone was okay with that. It was almost as though any opportunity to be together would have been acceptable. Terry placed her hand on Jake's thigh and said:

"We are so blessed."

"What did we do to get such terrific kids?" Jake added with a warm smile directed at each child.

Saturday morning came quickly. Jake loaded all of the materials needed in the back of his truck and headed off to the farm. Terry agreed to bring the children later. Upon arrival, Jake heard the sound of the trench digger, and the gate was open. As he neared the house, he saw Bob waiting.

"Who's running the trencher, Bob?"

"Brandon. If you show that kid anything one time, he thinks he is an expert." Bob laughed.

"I will unload the piping from my truck and meet you near the well."

The trench from the well to the barn was nearly complete. Brandon shut down the digging machine and began to clear what was left with a small spade. Bob had assembled a laundry tub, which Jake saw at the barn door.

"I thought we would run to a shutoff valve for now. I guess you went a step further?"

"There's always painting to do. I thought a laundry tub would serve us well. I also want a tap outside for watering."

"No problem. Place the tub where you want it. I will make all the connections."

The three men worked harmoniously together. Less than two hours later and even the trench was covered. Bob made a pot of coffee and brought out some pastries into the kitchen. He told Brandon to fetch some stools from the back of his truck to use around the island.

"So Jake, what do you think of your son?"

At first Jake thought he meant Matt and responded. Then something in Bob's voice said otherwise.

"So Brandon shared the news, huh?"

"He tried to, but I knew long before that."

With a puzzled look on his face, Jake replied, *"What do you mean?"*

"I brought you out here today to listen to a story, sort of a love story."

"Now I am really confused, Bob."

"Let me call it, "Bertha's Joy.""

"You aunt?"

"Yes, but she was more like a big sister to me. Anyway, she always wanted a big family. She only had one son and he died rather tragically in a car accident."

"How does that relate to Brandon or me?"

"Let me finish, Jake. Be patient. I can see that I caught you by surprise here. Long before her son died, Bertha began to have a real passion to help anyone in need, especially those involving children. She fostered over twenty children over the years."

"That explains it. I wondered how this house expanded with only one bathroom upstairs."

"I helped her many times to knock out walls and add more rooms over the years. The children never seemed to mind the limited bathroom space. They always made do and appreciated Bertha's help. She loved everyone who passed through her doors."

"So where does Brandon come in? Didn't he stay with his mother until she died?"

"Yes, he did. Both of them lived in this house for most of the last fifteen years. Brandon moved out after he graduated from high school. Bertha met Joy at the diner where she was a waitress. Brandon was three or four at the time. The bond between Bertha, Joy and Brandon became very strong. Joy felt secure, knowing that Bertha was caring for her son. They shared everything together, even up to her death."

"So how did you learn that I was Brandon's father?"

"Through Joy. She never forgot you and never remarried. When she started her battle with cancer, she desired to locate you and reintroduce you to your son. All we had to go on was some early pictures and your name. It took a while to find out that 'Jake' was a nickname for 'Jeremiah'."

"I haven't heard that name in many years."

"Eventually, I had a long talk with a judge, who was certain that the man I was looking for was you."

"Judge Carter?"

"That's him. I learned that you were working as a plumber's helper for a man named Joe."

"He helped me learn the business. Did you know that I married his daughter?

"I did. Nicole and Alicia are from that marriage as well. I had to learn a great deal about you, Jake. There were a lot of unanswered questions in Joy's head that needed answering. Each new piece of information was passed on as it was received."

"Must have sounded pretty bleak, huh? Prison, divorce, and a pretty mixed up life, I mean."

"I must admit it sounded pretty dim. Joy was not discouraged, however. She saw something in you that was good from the very beginning."

Jake sighed.

"The first time we ever met was at a gas station. You probably would not remember. I asked about the three crosses painted as a logo."

"A lot of people ask. I use it as my introduction to witness the love of Jesus Christ to them. People come and go, but you did look familiar when we first met at the site. Perhaps, that's where it came from."

"Very possible, Jake. But, I knew that you were a changed man that day. You spoke with the kind of peace that could only come from having a relationship with the very Prince of Peace. The life you had before that was about as opposite as it could have been."

"Now that we can agree on. Without Christ, I was one lost soul. Today, I consider myself a walking miracle."

"That you are, Jake. I think that Brandon feels much the same way today as well."

"So how did he turn out so great? He's quite a mature young man."

"Bertha always insisted on nurturing all who come under her roof to Godly principles. Everyone not only knew their responsibilities, but also respected the rights of each other. Church attendance was part of the deal. There were times when I needed to secure the church bus to get everyone there, but we did it."

"Aunt Bertha must have been a real gem. I only wish that I could have met her before she died."

"That she was."

"You told me that both Brandon and Joy received Christ and were baptized together. Could you tell me something about that?"

"I would like your son to share that part with you."

"Where is he? Didn't you send him out for stools? He should have been back by now."

"That was our little secret. I told him to wait until I called, before bringing them in. I wanted time to share with you alone>"

"Can you call him now?"

"That I can. Brandon, bring those stools in now, please."

Brandon had been waiting on the porch for nearly twenty minutes. He was sure about the topic of his uncle's conversation, so he did not enter the room with any element of surprise.

"So, Dad. Did uncle Bob get you all caught up?"

"He filled in a lot of blanks, son. From our earlier conversation, it sounded like he kept a lot from you as well."

"Well, I must say that I was shocked when I told him about you being my father. He knew all the time."

"I guess that he wanted you to find out for yourself, huh?"

"It was different for me. I liked you as a plumber. I mean that I wanted to learn your trade and you were willing to help. I also only knew you as a Christian man. I never knew much about your past."

"Now that you know more, are you less encouraged?"

"Are you kidding? I am even more excited to have you as my dad. You are a living miracle."

Jake was moved to tears. He could see pride written all over Brandon's face, which his words reflected. Images flashed in his memory of people who helped him along the way. It has been quite a journey. The son he had abandoned was now a man looking at his father with eyes of love and compassion. Jake felt much more than the love. He felt real forgiveness. He walked over to his son and embraced him like never before. It would be a hug that would bond them forever. Both men wept.

After a moment, Bob suggested that they have some pastries and coffee. All three men shared good times together, laughed, and occasionally shed a new tear. A few minutes later, Terry drove up with the kids. When they saw the food on the counter, they attacked it.

"You think that they have not been fed," Terry said, somewhat embarrassed. *"You kids should ask permission first."*

"That's okay. I brought the food to be eaten. Finish it up so we can go on a hayride. Is it okay if your mom and Brandon stay at the house? They have some things to discuss, kids," Bob asked.

"What things? Are any of those about us?"

"I assure you that they just need time together. It's not about you at all."

"Let's go riding." All were in agreement.

Jake filled in some of the blanks with Terry, while Brandon just listened. The idea that Bob knew all along stayed with Terry all day. Questions would surface about something that occurred days or weeks before, and new answers were applied just as quickly. It was as if God was orchestrating everything and everyone, right down to the smallest detail. The more the pieces came together, the more relief came as well, even for Brandon.

"Brandon, before Bob called you inside, I asked him to tell me about you and your mother's conversion experience. Can you share that with us now?"

"There was a lot going on at the time. Mom and I were attending church regularly, but the focus seemed to be on healing prayer. She had been diagnosed with cancer, and we both were praying for a healing miracle. Each week passed with less hope."

"That must have been hard on both of you," Terry inserted as she put her arm around Brandon.

"It was tough, but we believed that God would intervene. We hung on that promise. Mom's pain got increasingly worse. The medicines had reached their limit of effectiveness."

"You must have agonized with her," Terry said with emotion.

"The whole thing was way beyond anything I could handle, humanly. We knelt together one night at her bed and asked Jesus to come in to our hearts. First, I prayed. Then, mom began, but I sensed something that I don't think I felt before."

"What was that, son?" Jake asked.

"Great fear. Mom was so scared and ashamed. She broke her marital vows so long ago, and it had gnawed at her all those years. She actually felt that God was punishing her. She thought she deserved the pain."

Jake began to weep as Brandon spoke. He was caught up in the moment. He committed adultery and was as much of the problem as Joy was. Yet, she agonized over breaking a vow with God. At the time, Jake was about as far from his Creator as he possibly could be, so the sin had far less impact. As he listened, he could hear Joy's heart screaming for relief. Breaking a vow with God also broke her heart. They were two different people to be sure. Jake's tears also affected Terry, as she tried to embrace them both.

"So what happened next, Brandon?" Terry said after the tears slowed.

"She let go. I mean, mom let go of all of that anguish. She truly felt God's forgiveness for, perhaps, the first time in her entire life. The sin of adultery, which seemed so unforgivable, was just as suddenly forgiven. She gave her heart to Christ and it was miraculously cleansed. She was so different afterwards "

"Different?" Jake inquired.

"I should have said peaceful. Though her cancer took her, she left this world at peace."

"How did you feel when your mom died, Brandon?"

"I can tell you both that it was hard until I read the letter, the one you read in my homemade box.. Then I desired to find my real father. God has answered that prayer ten fold."

Terry, Jake and Brandon continued sharing for several hours. The presence of the Holy Spirit was felt along with great peace. Tears were mixed with laughter, and love was shared. Each heart had been on different journeys, but all roads came together to the old farmhouse.

The hayride ended and the children were hungry. Bob walked into the kitchen and could sense that genuine healing had taken place. He looked over at Brandon and said, *"I wish Aunt Bertha was here right now. She prayed for this moment."*

"She's smiling in heaven, Uncle Bob. There is great joy in that place, I am sure."

"I am sure as well." Brandon added with emphasis.

"Jake. Could you complete your bill and give it to me on Monday. I will meet you at the site and settle up. If you have it tomorrow at church, that would be even better."

"Sounds great, Bob. I am going to miss this place. Working here has been more fun than work. I think my children will agree with that."

THE SURPRISE

Terry invited Brandon back to their home for dinner, which was a special treat for Jake's entire family. Having Brandon in their home seemed to have a sense of completeness. For Jake, the journey God had been leading culminated in the reunion of his son. Jake recalled the parable of the "Wayward Son," where the son left by choice. This story was the opposite of Jake's life, as the one who chose to leave was Brandon's father. Still, the tremendous joy of their reunion left both men exhilarated. The fact that Brandon accepted his father with open arms was a miracle in itself.

Before going back to his apartment, Brandon was invited to join the Wilson family at church the next morning.

"We would love to have you attend with us, Brandon," Terry insisted. *"This family feels much more complete when you are among us."*

"Thank you, mom," Brandon gave an unmistakable look of love to Terry, and it was warmly received. *"I'll be there. I would love to spend more time with everyone as well."*

"We'll save a seat for you, son. Thanks for your help today. I will make sure that you are compensated."

"I already have been, Dad. Mom's cooking is second to none."

"You are always welcome in our home. It's your home, too, though a bit small. Perhaps, we will afford a home someday. If we do, we will keep a room available for you as well. That is of course, unless you want to keep your distance," Jake said, somewhat sarcastically.

"I always wondered what a 'Bed and Breakfast' place would be like. At least I would know that the food at your place would be worth the stay." Brandon returned the quip with a rather wide grin.

That evening, Jake and Terry began to share about the events of the day. Bob filled in a lot of blanks, and the farm's allure began to be less of a mystery. The day was filled with excitement, joy, peace, and wonderment. Both shared about the road they had traveled to reach this place in their lives, and how God had been with them all along. In many ways, their discussion sounded like a fairy tale conclusion, yet the idea of owning a home was still on the horizon for Jake. His family of four became one of six less than a year earlier. Now there were seven. The walls of the apartment seemed to be closing in. The dialogue continued well into the wee hours of the morning, until exhaustion took over. Hearts were shared, tears were shed, and sighs turned into blissful rest.

Terry arose to prepare breakfast at her normal time. Although, she only had a few hours of sleep, she felt energized and refreshed. There was joy at the Wilson home that morning, especially, with the anticipation that Brandon would join them at church. The van left a few minutes early, which was unusual to say the least. There were no last minute tasks yet to be done. Matt, Diana, Nicole, and Alicia were just as excited to see their brother as their parents were.

As usual, the children headed to their respective classes, while Jake and Terry headed to the coffee area. A moment later, Alex McDaniels spotted Jake and called out:

"Hi Jake. How's your week been?"
"Great, or even beyond great."
"You look like your feet are off the ground."
"I think they are. God is so good."

"You got that right. Anyway, I am glad that I caught you this morning. I looked into various home options for you since we talked last week."

"Your timing is pretty good, Alex. My family, officially, added a new member this week."

"How's that?"

God has brought my son to me, my first son from a failed marriage years ago. I tell you, God is awesome."

"That's wonderful, but your apartment must be busting."

"Yeah, well, Brandon is a young man and has his own place."

"Based on your needs, I have only a few options so far. A few banks may be interested in off-loading some foreclosed properties with the square footage that you need. These would need some restoration, due to the condition they were left in, but I know you can handle that. Down payments can be significantly reduced as a result."

"What does all that mean to me?"

"It means that we need to place your name in the hat to those banks and discuss your options further. Money for loans is the biggest problem, and solid credit is required for large loans. I will say that there are some great bargains out there due to the economic woes."

"So what are we talking about here? What will I need and how much will a mortgage be?"

"I worked out one scenario for you. This is a five-bedroom foreclosure in a good school location. The homes in the area go for three hundred thousand to nearly one million dollars. Yet, you may secure a loan for close to two hundred thousand with twenty-five down. To protect their investment, the bank may also cover the required materials. Work costs could easily constitute an additional down payment. Does any of this make any sense, yet?"

"Sort of. How much is a two-hundred thousand dollar loan going to cost me per month?"

"Roughly between eighteen hundred and two thousand, for a thirty year loan. Taxes also vary, but you can qualify as a first time homeowner, which will further reduce the burden."

"Thanks for the information. I will discuss it with Terry. She has been handling my financial affairs, and really done a great job. I have no idea where we stand, except that I need to find one more job like the farm to come up with the down payment."

"The farm?"

"That's a whole other story. I have to get off to class now. My son will join us for church as well. I hope you get the chance to meet him."

"I would like that as well. I'll talk to you later. Let the information sink in a bit with Terry for now, Okay?"

"Will do and thanks."

As Jake headed to his Bible study class, options of home ownership permeated his thought process. Hundreds of thousands of dollars weighted one side of the scale, while mortgage payments were on the other. Eighteen hundred dollars per month did not seem like a huge leap from his current rent, but the lesson of the ants from Terry seemed to place a warning sign to the concept of paying for thirty years. As much as Jake tried to concentrate on the lesson, home ownership concepts kept passing through his thought process.

Jake met Terry at the sanctuary entrance.

"How was your Bible study, Jake?"

"Fine, I guess. My mind was wandering a bit. Alex shared some things about mortgages before I went in, and they were still fresh on my mind."

"So, what did he say?"

"Homes are out there, especially foreclosures. We will need about twenty-five thousand dollars down and around eighteen hundred a month for thirty years. I guess that's the short version."

"We can talk about that later, but it sounds like another prayer concern."

"Okay. Have you seen Brandon, yet?"

"I haven't looked inside the sanctuary, but he has not appeared out here."

"Let's go inside and reserve seats. If we don't see him, I will come back out and wait."

As they entered the sanctuary, Jake felt a gentle tap on the shoulder. He turned and Brandon smiled.

"Brandon, how long have you been here? Jake inquired.

"About ten or fifteen minutes. I love to just listen to the preparation, especially the music. I like these moments of reflection."

"So are we in for a treat?" Terry said in response to the worship music.

"Praising God is always a treat. Having a heart ready to do that makes all the difference, regardless of the message or music."

"Well said, son. We usually sit towards the front. Is that okay with you?"

"You lead. I will follow, Dad."

Once again, Jake was moved by Brandon's words. The concept of being called a "Dad," had special meaning. There was a great deal of respect in the young man's words. He would follow his father's steps. This meant much more than a plumber's helper learning from the master. Those few short words took on the added significance of servanthood and obedience. It was also a tremendous responsibility for Jake. He pictured the long unbroken row of ants slowly and methodically moving towards one goal. There was unity of purpose. The fruits of their labor might not show for a season, but each ant pressed on. Jake silently prayed to the God who had walked in front of his journey of freedom:

"You lead, God. I will follow."

The thoughts of home ownership left and were replaced with a desire to worship. Jake could not wait to introduce his son to all he greeted. Pride was written on his face. It was a healthy pride, filled with love. Sunday afternoon was spent with the children at the apartment. Brandon could not say no to the offer of good home cooking, and the children were equally excited to spend time with their new brother. As everyone was leaving the church, Jake heard a familiar voice.

"Hey, Jake. Did you finish your bill for me?"

"I did, Bob." Jake pulled out a folded paper from his bible and handed it over. *"That should do it."*

"Thanks. I will see you tomorrow."

"You bet." The men parted company.

By the time the children were in bed and Brandon had gone back to his apartment, Jake and Terry were exhausted. With so much going on, Jake did not have time to discuss any details about home ownership possibilities. Instead, Jake embraced his wife and they prayed together.

Jake began. *"Dear Lord. You have led us this far and we are awestruck. This has been a journey that has taken each member of our family through some lows to enormous highs. You have answered every prayer and every dream beyond our wildest expectations. We give to you our heartfelt thanks for all you have done."*

Terry, lovingly, touched her husband as if to say, *"I am one with you."*

Jake continued. *"We will follow your lead into eternity, yet, you know we would like to have an earthly home large enough for our now extended family. We place that need at you feet right now and ask for direction. You are so awesome, Lord. We love you. Amen."*

The day was complete and rest came almost instantaneously. It was a day to remember, a day that placed a punctuation mark on the family relationship with Brandon.

The next morning, Jake anticipated his meeting with Bob. The money would go a long way towards a future home, but Jake was not ready for the surprise that awaited him. When he pulled into the work site, he heard the double beep from Bob's truck. Bob was eager to meet with Jake as well.

"Step into my office, Jake."

Bob had a small trailer set up at the construction site, which he referred to as his office. The two men entered. Bob left a map and some papers on a long table and motioned for Jake to sit down.

"Check out the map, while I put on a pot of coffee."

Jake sat down and pulled the map over for review. It appeared to be a layout for a new housing tract. Jake wondered if this would be a new source of work, yet there was something very familiar about the property. After a moment of pondering, he recognized two existing buildings and a winding creek as the ones at the farm.

"Is this your property, Bob? This looks like the barn and the house."

"That it is, Jake."

"The large acreage in the back looks like some new housing development."

"The housing contractor across the road, where we tapped into the water and sewer, made an offer on the property. I own about sixty acres. I sectioned the house and barn away, all the way to the creek. That left fifty-two acres for development I want the farmhouse and barn to stay as it is. The creek makes a great border don't you think?"

"With the tall trees around, you might not even see the new development, except after the leaves have fallen."

"The site map was being prepared by my lawyers. That was where I spent my time last Monday and Tuesday. I also needed to submit to the county board some zoning changes. I plan on selling the large portion to the development, but there is a stipulation."

"What's that, Bob?"

"I told them that I wanted you to be considered for all of the new development plumbing work. That should include Brandon as well, don't you think?"

"Easily. How did they respond?"

"Except for a few more signatures, it's a done deal my friend."

Bob could see the combination of emotions written on Jake's face. Bob was looking out for the Wilson family and that thought touched Jake's heart very deeply. Real men can cry, especially tears of joy. Jake could not hold them back. For several minutes no words were spoken. It just can't get any better than this, Jake thought. Then Jake gathered himself and asked:

"So are you going to sell the farm portion as well?"

"I have plans for that as well. Open the large envelope, Jake."

A large vanilla-colored envelope held several papers with legal mumbo-jumbo. Jake pulled the documents out and began to scan over them. The cover page listed the legal department information. The next page appeared to be a site map of the farm. Jake noticed the markings for the well, sewer, and water connection sites. As he sifted through the next several sheets, Jake's mind began to retreat to the months of time spent working on the property. The idea of selling it had been a reality, but these documents seemed to put closure to that possibility.

Then Jake looked at the final page. It was a deed, which looked far more professional than all of the other papers. It had a place for a raised seal, along with fancy script and distinguished lettering. The only thing close to that sheet, which Jake had some familiarity, was a car title. The document was impressive to view, as Jake seemed to just stare at it.

"So what do you think?"

"It's a bit more than my education can understand."

"Can you understand the name on the deed?"

Jake had not read very much of the wording, let alone the names. It all looked so professional. He scanned the document without paying attention to very much detail. Now he was asked to look, specifically, at the name on the deed. He looked down, and just as quickly looked up at Bob in disbelief.

"Those are our names. It says, 'Jeremiah and Terry Wilson. I, I don't understand."

"The lawyers seemed to think I should use your real name and not Jake." Bob said this as an icebreaker, as he could sense Jake was surprised.

"But, we don't own the property. Isn't that what a deed is for?"

"Actually, deeds are written for ownership, which could mean a lending institution until paid off by the borrower. So, technically, it is like a reservation for property"

"I was confused before and even more now. Why are our names listed on the deed?"

"Remember my story about Bertha's joy?"

"I do."

"I was the executor for her will. The property was placed in my name, but there was a clause. Bertha wanted the property to be used to help a family or families in need. That's why I had to keep the house separate from the rest of the land. I can see no greater joy in Bertha's heart than to look down from her place in heaven and see the fruits of her work, manifested in the earthly family living in her house."

"But, I cannot qualify for a loan, yet. Alex said I would need a lot more cash. I don't have any idea what the value of this farm even is, Bob."

"I have everything worked out, Jake. First, I am your banker. I will loan you the money. Second, The down payment comes to exactly what I owe you in labor charges, except for a small amount set aside for Brandon. Finally, I have only one request from you, but you need to talk it over with Terry."

"What's that?"

"Continue using the farm to help others, starting with Brandon. I'm sure he would like to move out of his apartment and use his chest of drawers."

"I am sure that he would as well. I can do all of that. In fact it would be an honor to continue Bertha's work. But you haven't given me the price, yet."

"I would like to propose a ten year note for six-hundred dollars a month, plus the cost of taxes and insurance. I believe the total would come to around one thousand dollars a month. How does that sound to you, Jake?"

"Too good to be true. Am I dreaming? Including interest, that is less than one hundred thousand dollars total."

"Actually, it covers all the fixtures, countertops, appliances, and other materials with a little left over. Bertha left enough to cover those costs, but since you will be enjoying them, I thought I would set up a fund for others in the future."

"But you could have sold the property for four or five times that amount. Are you sure that this is what you want to do?"

"This is what Bertha would want for me to do. When you follow God's leading, you cannot go wrong. You should have learned that by now. It all belongs to God. We are just caretakers. I desire for the words from heaven when I arrive to be 'Well done my good and faithful servant.'"

"Bob, you are amazing."

"No, my friend, it is God who is amazing. He has done great things in your life. Now you are destined to continue that work for others. If you can do that, you will have peace, Joy, and Oh Yeah, a roof over your head."

"Have you talked with Brandon about this?"

"No, Jake. There is one other thing, however."

"Here comes the big catch," Jake said with a wry smile.

"*I would like to keep Old Betsy and some things in the barn, along with the right to fire her up on occasion. I hope we can make that a gentleman's agreement.*"

"*That would be the least I can do. I'm still in a state of shock. Are you absolutely sure that you want to do this for us?*"

"*Jake. You need to examine your life and see how God has chosen you for a special task. You still have a long way yet to go, but Bertha, Joy, Brandon, and everything else is all part of that purpose. This is my part. I trust that God will bless my decision and your life. Now call that pretty wife of yours and share your excitement with her. Oh, when you do that, ask what's for dinner. You never know who might pop in.*"

"*I will call Terry, and you are always invited for dinner.*"

"*Take the legal papers with you. My lawyers have everything waiting for finalization. Read everything over and we will discuss a closing date to make things final. Share the news with Brandon at your own time.*"

Jake entered the trailer, expecting to leave with a check for services rendered. He left with a packet of papers and a dream fulfilled. Before he could attempt to complete the work he had laid out at the site, he had to call Terry. Thoughts about the discussion with Alex, relating to the cost of home ownership, resurfaced as well. There was no property in Alex's portfolio that could compare to the one just offered by Bob. Thirty years of debt was now ten years of love. Jake felt humbled and so very thankful.

Dennis A. McIntyre

The New Journey

*H*ello.

"*Terry, are you sitting down?*"

"*I'm washing a few dishes, honey. Do I need to sit?*"

"*You better, and take your hands off of any breakable items.*"

"*You don't sound like your news is anything bad. What's going on?*"

"*First, my news is not bad. In fact it's beyond anything either of us could have thought or dreamt. Second, I need to sit down to even share it with you.*" Jake sat in his cab and closed the door."

"*Jake Wilson. Tell me what's going on, already.*"

"*Honey, we are about to become proud home owners; I mean beyond our wildest dreams. The money I earned working for Bob was turned into a down payment for the house.*"

"*We can't afford that place. That money hardly makes a dent into its value.*"

"*I know. I know. But, it's a God thing. Bob wants the work that Bertha started to continue in her memory and we have been part of that work.*"

"*What do you mean?*"

"She has entertained the less fortunate, including over twenty foster children, my first wife, and Brandon. Bob also served as her executor. Finding Brandon's father and continuing the process of helping others was all part of her wishes. I am telling you, honey, it's a God thing."

Terry seemed to pause without any response.

"Honey, did I lose you. Can you hear me?"
"I'm here, Jake. I heard you. I just had a flashback for a moment."
"About what?"
"Lizards."
"Lizards? I must admit, I cannot see the connection."
"I think I do."
"You will have to explain that one to me, honey."
"Remember the lesson in proverbs about the ants? "
"You have been reminding me for several months. How can I forget?"

"At the end of that verse it talked about the wisdom of lizards living in palaces. Don't you see? Since both us came to know Christ, we have tried to stay close to His leading, much like the ants. I tried to apply that scripture to how we handle our finances, though I am sure that's important as well, and also wise. Can you picture a better palace than that old farmhouse?"
"No, I can't."
"Bertha entertained so many in need. They had no place of their own. Her home was like a palace to Joy, Brandon, and so many others. Bob wants to keep her dream alive."

"To think how many times I tried to keep the lizards out of the apartment," Jake winked.

"God has blessed Bertha's ministry in so many ways. She always desired a large family, though could not bear but one child. Even in that child's death, God gave her a new passion and purpose for

life. He has done that for our family as well. Nicole and Alicia were rescued from the alcohol and drugs of their mother."

"And Brandon has a permanent home as well," Jake added.

"I think that old farmhouse can hold one more family member." Terry said in agreement.

Jake held Terry's words dear to his heart. Somehow, a few verses of scripture, which seemed so out of place, took on new meaning. Jake had learned the lesson of letting go of the woes of his past and allowing God to direct his path. The journey led to an old farmhouse. Where it leads from there is a mystery. One thing is certain, however. When Jesus is doing the driving, then hang on for the ride.

Note from the author:
Dennis can be reached via email at
(dennismcintyre6@gmail.com)
and welcomes responses from readers.